PEL
THE BARBARIANS

P9-DMB-289

Ronald M. Berndt (M.A., Dip. Anthrop., Sydney; Ph.D., London) is Foundation Professor of Anthropology and head of the Department of Anthropology, in the University of Western Australia. His wife, Catherine H. Berndt (B.A., New Zealand; M.A., Dip. Anthrop., Sydney; Ph.D., London), is a part-time lecturer in the same Department. R. M. Berndt is General Editor of the journal *Anthropological Forum*; C. H. Berndt is an Assistant Editor. They met as students thirty-odd years ago and have continued together, up to the present time, the research in the Australian Aboriginal field on which he had already embarked. They have also carried out research in New Guinea. In the course of this they inevitably became concerned with studying the kind of society that has impinged on the indigenous people of those areas. They share a long-standing interest in Hindu-Buddhist iconography, and in 1965 they made a survey of Anthropology and related fields in India, for the Indian University Grants Commission. Their joint publications include *From Black to White in South Australia* (1951) and *Man, Land and Myth in North Australia. The Gunwinggu People* (1970).

THE
BARBARIANS

AN ANTHROPOLOGICAL VIEW

Catherine H. Berndt and
Ronald M. Berndt

PENGUIN BOOKS

Penguin Books Ltd, Harmondsworth, Middlesex, England
Penguin Books Inc., 7110 Ambassador Road, Baltimore, Maryland 21207, U.S.A.
Penguin Books Australia Ltd, Ringwood, Victoria, Australia

—

First published by C. A. Watts 1971
Published in Pelican Books 1973

—

Copyright © Catherine H. Berndt, Ronald M. Berndt, 1971

—

Made and printed in Great Britain by
Hazell Watson & Viney Ltd,
Aylesbury, Bucks
Set in Monotype Bembo

This book is sold subject to the condition
that it shall not, by way of trade or otherwise,
be lent, re-sold, hired out, or otherwise circulated
without the publisher's prior consent in any form of
binding or cover other than that in which it is
published and without a similar condition
including this condition being imposed
on the subsequent purchaser

Preface

WHEN we first began to think about writing this book we were excited at the prospect of combining several themes that have interested us, in different ways, for a long time.

One is the theme of civilization, or civilized living, or civilized man, in an age when more people are expressing uncertainty about the meaning of civilization and about human prospects for the future. (Of course, uncertainty is an inherent feature of the human condition – or, rather, insecurity, because the major certainties of that condition, in this world at least, are not such as to inspire confidence.)

In the course of ordinary conversations, we asked people of differing ages and occupations and educational status, etc., what they understood by 'civilization' – not as part of any organized survey with formalized sampling procedures, but largely to satisfy our own curiosity in the light of what we had heard and read about in other situations. The responses were, by and large, predictable. The commonest single answer was, 'living in cities' – but (when this was expanded) not just *any* city, and certainly not present-day New York, Chicago, San Francisco, Berlin, even London: in fact, no contemporary city, but rather the idea and the ideal of a city. Others emphasized reading and writing, science, technology and material comforts, and the realm of aesthetics, but bringing in negative as well as positive qualities. Others again contrasted European-type living and the great civilizations of Asia with the culture of non-literate ('primitive') peoples, including the Australian Aborigines.

One person combined 'Plato and the New Testament' as the twin pillars of Western civilization, but this kind of reply usually took the form of 'Well, I think of the Greeks', or, 'I think of the Romans'. It was expressed, however, in terms that reinforced an impression we had already received quite vividly from other sources – conversations and considered statements as well as written material. Interestingly, despite the emphasis on Greek contributions to the beginnings of science and of rational inquiry and on the Romans' secular achievements, attitudes regarding them were phrased in tones that were far from neutral. They had something of the quality of myth, using 'myth' in its time-honoured, anthropological sense: in this case, not myth of a highly sacred, religious kind, but nevertheless evincing to some extent the same aura of devotion and value-charged commitment.

In putting the volume together, we were attracted by several possibilities. One was to dwell on the philosophical and intellectual side of the argument, in Aboriginal Australia and New Guinea and in our own kind of society.

Another possibility was to omit the Aboriginal and New Guinea material almost entirely and concentrate on a single range of questions: '*Who* are the barbarians? From whose point of view, in what circumstances, and what kinds of interaction or cross-cutting influences were (are) involved?' Looked at in global or almost global time-and-space perspective, these have intriguing ramifications. They demonstrate clearly how multiple are the influences, none of them of a simple one-way kind, that have gone into the development of human cultures in general and 'civilizations' in particular. In the popular and negative sense, when the word 'barbarian' is used at all now, it seems to have the same connotation as its cognate, 'barbarous'. The answer to the question of 'Who...?' is simplified accordingly, and takes on varying associations of 'scapegoat' or 'vandal'. For some, the answer is 'politicians', as formally responsible for initiating actions or implementing policies that are 'unpopular' or 'ill-considered' or 'against the real interests' of a nation. For others, the answer is 'drop-outs' and 'junkies', or 'plane hijackers', or 'gangsters'—on the grounds that they evade or defy established rules or laws or moral codes. Or the answer is *all* of us' – in so far as we fall short of ideal standards of civilized or humane behaviour, or fail to contribute to advancing 'civilization' a little further, or make no attempt to stem its decline. And so on. But this is not a political book. Nor is it a book about morals or ideals.

Given our particular background of interests, discussing civilization had to mean discussing Aborigines and New Guinea people too – because they have so often been cited as a contrast: as *un*civilized, even savage. And so, that is one facet of our main theme – the topic of civilization versus something else.

The content of Part II relates to another facet of that theme, one that we foreshadowed in talking about attitudes to the classical world of Greece and Rome. This is the 'middle range' of myth and symbolic language – in between the sacred and the mundane, but merging into these at either end.

In myth, we are dealing with value-charged commitment and belief that belong pre-eminently to the field of religion and the non-empirical but spill over into other spheres. A great deal of debate has gone on about the relationship between religion, magic and science and the usefulness of distinguishing, or not distinguishing, between them. The same thing applies to categories like rational and non-rational, and to the question of the place of values in scientific research and in the use of its findings. Whatever criteria we employ in defining these concepts, and however relativistic our position in that respect (e.g. 'Who's to say what rationality is? It depends on the socio-cultural context!'), some sort of contrast is involved. Changing the labels or the boundaries does not dissipate or resolve the issues. This is not so much a contrast between the objective, universalistic, ideal values of science and the more emotional values that underlie humane or humanitarian considerations – relevant as that contrast is, in the current world scene. It is a contrast between science as, ideally, neutral and uncommitted to socio-cultural alignments and ideologies, and myth as, virtually by definition, anything *but* neutral.

Symbolic language, on the other hand, is the language of analogy and metaphor, the figurative expressions that are inseparable from speech and writing and the so-called visual arts in all human societies. Like other types of language, this represents *code* rather than *content*. It can be used to convey almost any kind of message. It is a part of civilization in the broadest sense, and also of a process that is sometimes identified with this but sometimes regarded as its opposite, i.e. the process of modernization.

From early in 1956, one of us (C.H.B.) had begun to collect examples of press and other cartoons and advertisements, as part of a larger interest in mass media which came out of a long-standing concern with myth – and with interpersonal communication in a variety of settings, in the oral tradition of the non-literate world, in folk songs and 'pop' songs (content and context) and in the two-pronged commercial and quasi-personal appeals of some radio and television networks.

One stimulus to looking more closely at the blend of old and new in various mass media, a blend we had documented more consistently in Aboriginal Australian and New Guinea mythology, was a Vicky *Evening Standard* cartoon reproduced in the Australian press in 1961. Looking out from a small wooden boat in a stormy sea is a group of animals and birds with the faces of contemporary politicians: Adenauer (vulture), Macmillan (sad lion-face), De Gaulle (giraffe), John Kennedy (eagle), Khrushchev (giant panda?), Mao (rabbit?),

Ulbricht (bison? buffalo?), and above them all a Nehru-dove bearing an olive branch. The caption reads: ' "Communists and capitalists alike, we are like the animals Noah took on board. If we fight each other we will destroy the ark, this earth of ours." / Mr. Khrushchev, July 3, 1960.'

What appealed to us here was the way the message was framed – the Animal-Farm style of analogy in the framework of an old, traditional Biblical story, providing a topical statement in a mass medium. There are of course thousands of such examples, drawing on different stories and themes, not only in cartoons but in advertising as well. The symbolic language that is one of their hallmarks mixes old and new, traditional and modern. It is conservative *and* innovative. Cartoons use symbolic language to comment graphically on issues of the day, and some comic strips do this too. The most sophisticated of them in substance and in skill of presentation are a significant part of the documentary record of local, national and international history. Advertisements, however, use symbolic language as a weapon in the competitive sphere of the market place. Both of them reflect, and perhaps help to perpetuate, colloquial speech and changing conventional styles. We would have liked to say more about all this, and about truth and falsity and ideas of 'reality' in the mass media: about 'justifiable hyperbole' or 'legitimate puffery' in advertising, for example, and public identification of film and fictional characters as 'real'. No one who is interested in the symbols of our time, including transient symbols, can fail to be interested also in the language of advertising, wherever it appears – however mundane or un-symbolic it may sometimes seem. And much of this belongs, essentially, within the context of persuasion, propaganda, social and political influence and counter-influence: the field of social communication and interaction in which myth, and 'mythical thinking', are particularly pertinent.

In Parts III and IV, then, we continue with our main theme: we are concerned with some of the ingredients of civilization, and also with the contrast between civilization and something else. But in this case, the 'something else' is not the external world of so-called tribal people. It is built into the fabric of contemporary living in what has for a long time been conventionally known as the civilized world. Here, increasing rejection of traditional values and increasing doubts about the outcome have a parallel, on a smaller scale, in the situations we touch on in Part II – the 'shake up' that the indigenous peoples of Australia and New Guinea experienced, in an enforced confrontation between a familiar past and an unfamiliar future. Uncertainty, conflict and clashes of interest, protests, manoeuvring for political and economic and social advantage, are present in some degree in any society. But in times of rapid change they are intensified, and myth – myth in the negative sense – becomes especially important.

Unsettlement and upset are the rule rather than the exception in human affairs. Definitions of civilization are not so much statements about observed reality. Rather, on the basis of material and other indexes, they point to achievements that have so far been only incompletely realized. In the very narrow field of techniques and technology, we can speak of 'accomplishments' with fewer qualifications than in other respects, but definitions resting on that dimension alone are correspondingly narrow. The 'technology index' is quite inadequate on its own. In so far as we can speak of progress in the direction of civilized living, we must certainly draw our examples from a wider range of human societies than those that are all too glibly referred to under that heading; and instead of 'civilized societies' it is more useful to single out specific aspects that can be so labelled. But whichever items we choose, we cannot fail to recognize how precarious such 'progress' is – how easily, for instance, any small gains toward a wider appreciation of 'humanity' can be opposed and reversed.

So much reading has gone into the preparation of this book, so much material has been collected, that in its present form it is now a modest shadow of a rather more ambitious design. We hope that in the whittling-down process we have not omitted too much that would be helpful in an introductory statement, which is what this is now. We don't pretend to have done more than touch on the subjects we discuss. We have tried to cover a fairly wide field, and in so doing we have brought together a number of topics that are not usually juxtaposed in quite this way. Discussions of civilization, for instance, tend to focus on larger designs, larger issues, while the content of mass media appears under other headings or between other covers. Similarly with material on tribal peoples, on the nonliterate world, except in so far as they are drawn into expositions of evolutionary and other schemes concerned with 'civilization'.

Our field research in Aboriginal Australia has extended over a very long period, since we first worked together in the Great Victoria Desert of South Australia in 1941, and it was supplemented by almost a year in New Guinea. We must acknowledge the assistance of the various institutions, etc., which contributed to this, in terms especially of research and typing funds: the former Australian National Research Council, the University of Sydney, the International Federation of University Women (for C. H. Berndt's part of our New Guinea fieldwork), the University of Western Australia, the Australian Institute of Aboriginal Studies, and the Australian University Grants Commission.

Not least, our thanks to Mr T. M. Schuller. His kindly and mostly patient forbearance has survived the long delay since the idea of the book was first broached. We hope that the finished product justifies his faith in it. Knowing what we

have been obliged to omit, we can only say that we have
enjoyed writing it and we trust that others will enjoy reading
it.

The University of Western Australia

Catherine H. Berndt
Ronald M. Berndt

Contents

List of Illustrations

(*between pages 92 and 93*)

A symbolic statement from India

Tradition and modernization

Advertising for Adults

A symbolic statement in a topical cartoon

PART 1

CIVILIZATION—
SOME POINTS OF VIEW

1
The Greek Myth*

MANY of us whose cultural origins lie in Western Europe, wherever our homes are now, were exposed quite early to what could be called (if we allow this contradiction in terms) a secular-religious belief – secular in content, in that it had little to do with deities or the supernatural or with religion in the conventional sense, but religious in quality. Faith, fervour, devotion are not inappropriate words here. Those of us not directly caught up in this belief and the practices associated with it, even those indifferent or hostile to it, nevertheless grew up in its shadow.

In essence, it was this: that the culture of classical Greece was superior, not only to everything that had gone before it but also to much, perhaps most, of what came after it; that it represented an achievement in civilization which, techno-

* 'Myth' in the conventional anthropological sense, with a positive connotation. See Chapter 7.

logical developments notwithstanding, has remained virtually
unequalled in human history. This view was maintained with
such assurance and supported by such a formidable weight of
scholarship that it was not easily challenged. And any opposition was already accounted for in advance on the grounds that
it was, more or less by definition, a sign of ignorance or
prejudice. Adopting this Graeco-centric orientation and taking
steps to perpetuate it, by learning if not actually teaching
it – these were, in fact, the hallmarks of a truly 'educated'
person.

Greek specialists conceded some merit to studies focusing on
ancient Rome, as part of the classical tradition, but not to the
extent of according them equal status. The widespread use of
Latin as an academic and ecclesiastical language, the language
of an educated person, did not affect this evaluation. From the
standpoint of scholars dedicated to the memory and the
continued transmission of the culture of classical Greece, what
the Romans had to offer was a derived, secondary culture, not
to be compared with the original.* To some of them, indeed,
the ancient Greeks were – and are – closer and more real than
their living contemporaries.† They saw the world through
Greek eyes. Consciously or otherwise, their ideas of good and
bad, and their sense of human possibilities and limitations,
rested on their vision of Greece in its heyday. All that was
good in Western Europe stemmed from that small area in

* Greek culture has been called that, too. Braidwood, looking
beyond it to western Asia, once spoke of Greece 'as a second degree
derived civilization'. R. J. Braidwood, *Prehistoric Men*, Scott, Foresman
& Co., Glenview, Ill., 1967 (seventh ed.), pp. 154–5.

† P. H. Robins, *A Short History of Linguistics*. Longmans, 1967, p. 10,
suggests that it is not only scholars who feel more of an affinity with the
Greeks than with any other people, present or past: he sees this as a
bond between the Greeks and 'modern man'. Others have said the same,
for different reasons, about Catullus – 'most human' of all the Roman
poets, who speaks to us so directly across 2,000 years.

the Aegean, at a time between the Dark Ages (i.e. before the development of writing) and the fourth century B.C. It fired their imagination and stimulated their devotion to an extent no human culture has been able to achieve – not so consistently, nor on so large a scale. And, more than the glamour of ancient Egypt or the marvels of Babylon (for instance), it was part of their own cultural genealogy, their own cultural 'family tree'. Some anthropologists become so engrossed in their particular fieldwork areas that almost everything they say professionally, and non-professionally too, is slanted in that direction: 'My people' (whoever they are) 'don't do this, they do that', etc. So, others who have been deeply enough immersed in Greek or Roman studies use these cultures as their frame of reference in looking outward at others. It is, for them, the equivalent of the anthropologist's cross-cultural experience with living peoples, and carries with it something of the same dilemma: the need to steer a middle course between insufficient involvement, i.e. remaining simply an 'outsider', and too deep a concern with an 'inside' view, resulting in emotional and intellectual *over*-commitment to it.

In the last few years, however, emphases in school and university curricula have been changing. As Robert Graves,* among others, has pointed out, even a reasonably well educated person can no longer be expected to know the names of the main Greek mythical and other characters that he would once have taken very much for granted.

The use of Latin has been shrinking, too. Its association with power and privilege based on birth, whether these connections are real or imputed, are a disadvantage in an age that is becoming more accustomed to other styles of social inequality. And in this new climate of opinion, it has been vulnerable to the charge that it is not sufficiently relevant to

* In *The Greek Myths*, Vol. 1, Penguin Books, 1955, p. 9.

practical issues. The Church* has been its last real stronghold outside the schools and universities. But even there it has yielded ground, to meet the demand for direct communication with congregations in their own vernacular languages. In the fairly neutral field of scientific classification, supplemented by Greek, it continues to serve as an international code – but as a vocabulary or series of vocabularies rather than as a language in its own right.

The same quasi-democratizing† processes that have militated against it in other directions have been eroding another of its long-standing functions. In the secular sphere as well as in the sacred, it continued in use for a very long time as a distinct language, although a specialized one. Material that was otherwise not conventionally acceptable in written form could be put politely in Latin: Latin, somehow, made it respectable. Most of this was on sexual themes, ostensibly handled in a sober, scientific way but still regarded as far too strong for the ordinary reader. As to *who* regarded it in that light – both official and unofficial censorship was involved. In Latin dress, such material could be published or distributed with less risk of being officially banned. Scholars who had grown up in that particular tradition tried to see that it was maintained, to the extent of putting mild pressure on some anthropologists carrying out research among peoples who were reputed to be less reticent on sexual matters than, say, middle-class Euro-

---

* Helen Waddell, in *The Wandering Scholars*, Penguin (Pelican) Books, 1954 (1st pub. 1927), p. 17, noting the church's continued concern with teaching the classics, reminds us 'that but only for the church, the memory of them would have vanished from Europe'. So does Robert Graves, op. cit., p. 9.

† quasi, because 'democracy' covers a range of quite disparate social and political arrangements. These rest, not so much on discrepancies between ideal and actuality, as on differences between ideals themselves. There is no universal consensus, either on what democracy ought to be in the contemporary world or on how best to achieve it.

peans were. (At the time of our early fieldwork in Aboriginal Australia, one older European colleague insisted to us that Latin was the only proper medium for reporting on topics like marital and extra-marital relations.)

In the so-called permissive society of the late 1960s and early 1970s the idea of any kind of censorship, oblique or otherwise, is under fire. The opinions of the 'silent majority' are not clear on this point. But the noisiest demands call for a completely open society, one in which nothing is officially secret and no official arbiters of taste or morals are in a position to impose their judgement on others. Here, too, the stress is on the vernacular – on direct communication in the local language of the people, whatever that may be, in contrast to the specialized code of an élite minority.

In short, an account of the changing use of Latin in Western Europe and its cultural outliers would be, in essence, an account of the changes that have taken place through time in its socio-cultural context.

So many divergent strands have gone into the making of the Western European tradition that its content cannot be compressed into a few words, even in outline. Strictly speaking, of course, it comprises not one but a multitude of traditions, that vary a great deal, both in their regional spread and in the degree of importance attached to them by local people and by outsiders. It is enough for our purpose here to remember that there are also significant continuities and similarities. And in one sense, like the mythological heritage of many of the world's peoples, this has crystallized in an assortment of beliefs and ideas that look back to a Golden Age in the past and provide a charter for social and personal identification in the present.

It was quite natural for Western European scholars to frame their charter-of-origin in European terms. Smaller local groupings within the overall span labelled 'Europe' looked inward to their own specific traditions as a basis for national or regional unity. But the overarching connections between them that transcended local differences and gave shape to the idea of Europe *as* Europe, had their source in the influence of Rome – and so, distantly and indirectly, of Greece. Religious myths like that of the Garden of Eden purport to account for the creation of man as a physical being, but a physical being endowed with a soul. The findings of prehistoric archaeologists describe the development of man-the-toolmaker. But the Greek Myth points to the creation of rational man.

The dwindling number and range of channels for the formal transmission of Latin and Greek, and of the classics generally, have not diminished the enthusiasm of their advocates. On the contrary. In a world where many traditional values have been shaken, the Greek Myth points backward to a Golden Age, to an era that seemed to herald a breakaway from the emotionally charged partisan world of mythical thought. That era marked the beginnings of a rational, more or less impersonal approach to human beings and their natural environment, one that involved not simply the specifics of scientific procedure, but the impartial, open-ended inquiry that is the essence of the scientific method. Many present-day academic disciplines acknowledge 'founding ancestors' there, and not only those in the physical and mathematical sciences. If Thucydides is the 'father of History' – history as an objective record of past events* – so is Herodotus. But Herodotus is also a 'father' of Geography (he reported events in space) and of Anthropology (he was interested in other socio-cultural situations as well as his own, and endeavoured to make the foreign and the exotic intelligible to his readers).

In some respects there are obvious parallels between that

* J. Goody and I. Watt, 'The Consequences of Literacy,' in J. Goody, ed., *Literacy in Traditional Societies*, Cambridge University Press, 1968, p. 47.

age and the present, if only in the excitement of intellectual discovery. This too is a time of questioning and reassessing, of looking again at accepted beliefs and assumptions. But today's world is, simultaneously, both wider and smaller. Wider, in the expanding awareness of different ways of life. Smaller, in that technical improvements in transport and communications have brought dramatic changes in the time-space ratio, former strangers have suddenly become close neighbours, and what happens to any one group of people is increasingly relevant to others. Even the largest of earlier population movements and migrations in human history lacked the variety of cultural ingredients and the global range of contacts that are an intrinsic part of the contemporary scene. And the fact that written and orally-recorded material on all of this is continuously available adds a further dimension to it. Documentary and archaeological and other evidence from a vast array of sources is drawn upon, interpreted, and reinterpreted in a never-ending flow of often contradictory statements.

The aftermath of two world wars, the continuing incidence of smaller ones, and frequent references to the possibility of an even more devastating third, plus the widespread incidence of civil disturbances, complicate the scene, in a tangled interrelationship of causes and consequences. They have rendered more complex a process that, in itself, is far from new. It is a feature of all human situations. In defining their particular social and personal identities, people everywhere have considered themselves in relation to others, highlighting similarities or contrasts: and, in so doing, they have looked at their own past from the vantage point of the present, reshaping and selecting from their available information on it. To many of them, whether or not they have spelt it out explicitly, the only real meaning of the past lies in its bearing on the present. This is not history-as-a-record-of-past-events, but the more obviously selective variety: history-as-myth, serving the interests of a given people at a given point in time.

The growing mass of information on the past and the present of the world's populations reads like an encyclopaedia of human possibilities. In conjunction with optimistic assertions of freedom and individual self-determination, it might seem to present a tempting array of choices. But in actuality the possibilities are limited – and not only by economic and political considerations, although they are perhaps the most conspicuous.

In earlier days, outside their respective homelands, both Greek and Latin afforded to educated persons a vista of expanding horizons, cutting across specific local perspectives. They did this, not so much through their content, significant as that was, nor through the contact that they made possible with people and customs of the past. Above all, each in its time supported a network of *social* relationships, forging links between living people through the medium of a common language and all that this implied. They extended the bases of communication across regional and cultural boundaries, even though the impetus to this expansion stemmed from military or commercial or religious endeavour, with the interests of pure scholarship playing a subordinate role.

This has certainly a familiar ring. The same kinds of context are still relevant in the intermingling of different populations. But other circumstances and other outlooks, while they were certainly present before, have become more important. For an educated person *now*, the task is far more onerous. Ideally, he should be able to meet the challenge of expanding horizons with a fuller and deeper appreciation of peoples who were little more than names, if that, to his ancestors of only a few generations back. Ideally, this appreciation should extend beyond the larger and politically powerful nation states to what one social scientist has called*

* P. E. Slater, 'Social Bases of Personality,' in N. Smelser, ed., *Sociology: an Introduction*, Wiley N.Y., (International edition), p. 559.

'small tribes with negligible cultures'. They are also part of his world, even if he never comes into direct first-hand contact with any of them or any of their traditional manifestations. They are among the 'others' he must take into account in coming to terms with his own social and personal identity. For some people who have dealings with foreign or alien cultures, this feedback into their own local situation, whether or not they put it in quite that way, is the main if not the only justification for the effort. ('What can he know of England, who only England knows?')

A number of anthropologists who focus on research in societies other than their own see this as more than a mere by-product: 'By understanding other societies and cultures, we come to have a better understanding of our own'. Others do not accept it in that light: 'By understanding other societies, we come to know more about *all* human behaviour' – with all that this involves in the search for generalizations, principles, or laws. But if understanding is an ultimate goal in both cases, they are actually expressing almost the same thing. Notwithstanding all we have been saying, however, only the most obstinate extremists propose a complete substitution for studies of classical Greece and Rome. To persons whose background is preponderantly or even partially European, there is some continuity here: a sense of the sequence of events and shaping of identities – and, above all, a sense of *change*. The widening of choices in educational programmes may prove an advantage here. Faced with the loss of large 'captive' classes of schoolchildren, writers on these topics must compete for the attention of their readers: and the growing attractiveness of such studies* is perhaps one consequence of this. Adults who are no longer burdened with dreary memories of the more tedious sections of the Trojan or Persian wars, or

* For example, the volumes on aspects of Greek and Roman society in the various Penguin (Pelican) series.

Caesar's exploits in Gaul, are much less likely to be repelled by the thought of reading anything in that field. More than that, they may well be drawn to discover, or re-discover, it. And this is made easier now, by accounts that are set more obviously within a broader context of parallel studies, alongside others, and not the province of a specialized élite.*

* A 'revised version' of the Greek Myth, in that sense, is G.S. Kirk's study, *Myth. Its Meaning & Functions in Ancient and Other Cultures*, Cambridge University Press & University of California Press, 1970. (It appeared while this book was in press.) Its strength lies in its analysis of the development of Greek mythology and rational thought in the light of outside influences. On the score of myth in general terms it is less successful – not so much because of the author's conviction that literacy brings about fundamental changes in myth as such (and he talks about primitive, 'savage' societies), but because, after so many Olympian pronouncements in the course of his discusssion, his final comments come as very much of an anti-climax.

2

Barbarians and Savages

THE dialectic between the familiar and the strange, between home and abroad, is a universal one. 'East, west, home's best', and so on – but 'Over the road the grass is greener'. The content of the dialectic varies even within one society, according to time and circumstance and according to the social units and the individual persons concerned. Whatever the general trend, not everyone conforms with it, except under duress (e.g. conscription in war, or in refugee conditions, and the like). In every society there are people who prefer to stay at home and listen to travellers' tales (or watch them on television), and travellers who move out beyond the bounds of their own social environment to see something of others.

One powerful incentive to 'move out' is trade. On a small scale, it is another cultural universal, one known to be present in all human societies. The question, 'What is universal in human culture or experience or physical make-up, and what is more localized or personal?' is probably at the heart of both the sciences and the humanities. When it is posed directly, as mostly it is not, one approach is to focus on a specific topic. For example, some anthropologists have singled out the nuclear family of father, mother and child and asked, 'Is this family unit universal?' – meaning, 'Is it sufficiently similar everywhere, in form and content, to be spoken of in that way?

Or are some cases too divergent, as in the Israeli kibbutz and South Indian Nayar situations?' Another approach is to attempt a list of socio-cultural universals. This was particularly popular a few years ago. One attraction was the hope of being able to define the idea of normality on a universal basis, and the related possibility of arriving at a universally valid moral and ethical code. Clyde Kluckhohn's name stands out here.*

With smallness of scale goes something else – a more personalized orientation, and the feeling that material goods are not the whole substance of the transaction. This is why anthropologists like Marcel Mauss and, later, Lévi-Strauss have drawn attention to similarities between exchange of goods in the non-literate world, and the giving of presents in, say, European-type societies. What they have in common is not just the notion of balance or reciprocity, but this feeling that to treat it as *only* an exchange of material things would do violence to the social relationship involved. There are, of course, varying degrees of formality, even in regard to simple gift-exchange on an interpersonal basis. And this is more obvious in group enterprises, such as (to cite two New Guinea examples) the elaborate cycle of the *kula* ring linking the Trobriands and adjacent islands, that Malinowski first made famous, and the trading voyages of *lakatoi* sailing-canoes that went to and fro across the Gulf of Papua from near what is now Port Moresby.

In more impersonal settings, the 'gift-exchange' aspects of trade become submerged under the economic and commercial aspects. Of course, this is a discussion in itself, with all sorts of ramifications. Even if we were to look no further than small-scale societies, we would have to consider an enormous diversity of empirical cases. One has only to think of the 'potlatch' of the Kwakiutl Indians of the north-west coast of

* See, for example, his article in A. L. Kroeber *et al.*, eds., *Anthropology Today*, University of Chicago Press, 1953.

North America, where a man would ritually destroy property he himself had accumulated, to shame his rivals in the struggle for prestige and challenge them to go one better. ('Fighting with property', one anthropologist has called it.*) It might seem unnecessary to speak of *socio*-economic affairs, because the label 'economic' has little meaning unless it relates to the social dimension – in short, to people. The potlatch kind of example helps to remind us of this.

Our point here is the place of trade, broadly interpreted, in relations between peoples, whether such peoples are neighbours or, at least to begin with, strangers. It was the force that propelled so many European explorers and adventurers, lured by dreams of the 'wealth of the Indies', or other more (or less) realistic versions of the 'pot of gold at the foot of the rainbow' idea. And one result of such enterprises, large and small, was the introduction and circulation of new goods – including new foods.

Some anthropologists have concentrated on this fascinating field of diffusion of tangible and intangible things, between and within societies, the acceptance (or rejection) and modification of 'new' goods and ideas. North American ethnologists (the branch of cultural Anthropology concerned with 'culture history') like Clark Wissler looked at the distribution of various traits and trait-complexes, and drew tentative conclusions about previous, undocumented contacts between the people who shared them in the contemporary scene. The 'culture circle' school based on Vienna under men like Schmidt and Koppers was concerned with the same kind of problem, rather differently interpreted. Elliott Smith and Perry suggested past connections between Middle America and ancient Egypt. The best-known interpretations and

* Helen Codere, *Fighting with Property*, Augustin, Seattle, 1950. (Anthropologists who have reported on this spectacular property-burning rite included Franz Boas.)

experiments, however, are probably those of Thor Heyerdahl, who has brought into popular focus the possibility of early population contacts between South America and Polynesia. Hundreds of other scholarly and not-so-scholarly inquiries and theories have taken up the question of interconnections between peoples, where no written documents are available to fill in gaps in our knowledge about them, and also where such documents as there are do not supply enough evidence on that score. Translated into different operational language and a different academic research climate, this is the field of innovation (and innovators) versus conservatism. And one of its paths leads directly into the arena of consumer advertising, opinion research, the effects of mass media versus interpersonal influence in regard to what people buy and say and do, how they respond or don't respond to pressures exerted on them from a multitude of sources (see Chapter 9).

Warfare, and religious pilgrimages and missionary enterprises, provided opportunities for the movement of goods (as well as for their destruction), but of course these had other implications too. And some voyages and other events leading to inter-group contacts appear to have been accidental. The Polynesians, for instance, were great voyagers and skilful navigators. But over and above the long-distance war and raiding and trading expeditions they engaged in, like other Pacific peoples, and the banishment of individual offenders who were sent off in small craft to almost certain death, traditions tell of canoes missing their hoped-for landfall or drifting far off course to unknown destinations. The early colonization of New Zealand, by waves of Moriori and then Maori settlers, is the subject of many such oral traditions (supplemented, in 'historical' times, by archaeological evidence). Small vessels from the Indonesian archipelago still land occasionally on the north coast of Australia, carried there by the north-west monsoon – thus partially corroborating

Aboriginal traditions of shipwrecked travellers from foreign places 'speaking the language of birds'. And such episodes could be repeated on a world-wide basis.*

This brings us to one of the most important, if not *the* most important, criteria for assessing sameness and difference, identifying the range within which a person can talk of 'we' versus 'they'. Appearance, what people look like, is undoubtedly significant. Speech, however, is even more so. Mutual intelligibility is a key issue. Sharing the same language means more than sharing a code of sounds: it means sharing a world of understanding – though not, necessarily, of agreement. This applies also when 'the same language' consists of a number of dialects, in a traditionally bilingual or multilingual situation (as in north-eastern Arnhem Land, in Aboriginal Australia: see Chapter 4). In such a situation – and remember the provision, 'traditionally bilingual or multilingual' – dialect divisions emphasize differences *within* a common framework of assumptions and ideas. It is one level of the 'we-they' contrast, but a minor level. This contrast is always relative. Even within the immediate family, to spell this out, the 'we' of husband-and-wife is not the 'we' of father-and-son, or mother-and-daughter; and all of them together may be 'we' in contrast to someone else, or another family. (Some languages go a little further than English in specifying levels of inclusiveness. For example, in parts of both Aboriginal Australia and New Guinea, a speaker uses one word for 'we' if the action referred to includes the person addressed and another if it does not. These words also vary for number, usually between a dual form, 'we two', and an ordinary plural.)

* An interesting example, which throws light on relations between China and Korea in the Ming Dynasty, is the narrative of a shipwrecked Korean: J. Meskill, *Ch'oe Pu's Diary: A Record of Drifting across the Sea*, Mon. of the Ass. for Asian Studies, Vol. XVII, University of Arizona Press, 1964.

Linguistic differences, then, can be a basis for asserting differences in social and personal identity – and vice versa. They can be magnified to reinforce feelings of difference that rest on other grounds. But, the greater the perceived divergence in language, the greater this feeling of social difference? And does social distance mean social separateness? Not necessarily.

Scales designed to measure social distance can be helpful, provided they discriminate between two interrelated facets of it. The hostility–friendship scale is not identical with the perception-of-closeness–perception-of-distance scale, and these two need not coincide. Relationships of enmity between neighbouring groups (or neighbours) can be just as close as relations of friendship* – whereas faraway strangers who pose no threat may be regarded with indifference, which may show up more positively than this on attitude-scales. Once we start asking questions about content (*what* is being measured), we have to go further and ask about procedures (*how* the person who is doing the measuring sets about it). And this leads into the wider issue of social scientific method – which we take up, briefly, in Chapter 7.

Finer distinctions aside, there is plenty of evidence to show that, from the standpoint of 'insiders' looking outwards, linguistic criteria loom very large indeed. As the saying goes, 'the Greeks had a word for it' – in this case, 'bárbaroi'. Maybe this was, as some writers have suggested, a neutral word, not deliberately intended to be derogatory: but the implication is there. And that implication comes through more forcefully in the form in which it has passed into English – 'barbarian'.

It was Tylor who popularized this word in Anthropology, in his threefold scheme for classifying all humanity. Mankind,

* For a New Guinea example, see R. M. Berndt, *Excess and Restraint*, Chicago University Press, Chicago, 1962.

he said,* could be 'roughly classed into three great stages, Savage, Barbaric, Civilized'. 'The lowest or savage state is that in which man subsists on wild plants and animals'; men reach the barbaric stage when they 'take to agriculture' or use animal herds as a source of milk and meat; 'civilized life may be taken as beginning with the art of writing, which . . . binds together the past and the future in an unbroken chain of intellectual and moral progress'.

What Tylor was trying to do was to establish a sound basis for evaluating and comparing peoples, one that would be both objective and scholarly. His classification (and note that it rested on the idea of *stages*) leaned very heavily on 'hard' data, and especially on the kind of data that has sometimes been regarded as the hardest of all, i.e. economic data. For Gordon Childe, who adopted the same classificatory scheme but in a more elaborate and sophisticated style (and traces his ancestry in this respect further back, to Morgan rather than to Tylor), such data provided the central criteria. In Childe's transition from savagery to barbarism, too, food-cultivation was a necessary step, the beginning of what he called 'the neolithic revolution' – and so to the production of a food surplus, and eventually to urbanization, to a specialized division of labour, to writing, and to civilization. Of course, this is over-simplifying his argument, which is thoughtfully and carefully developed – and has had an enormous influence, not merely on archaeologists and culture-historians but also (it seems) on popular thinking. It has helped to reinforce still-current views of Aborigines as 'modern savages'.†

Other writers before and since Childe have tried to develop a framework of categories based on economic criteria alone.

* E. B. Tylor, *Anthropology. An Introduction to the Study of Man and Civilization*, Macmillan, 1881, p. 24.

† For example, Gordon Childe, *What Happened in History?* Penguin Books, 1942/1967: with a new Foreword by Grahame Clark.

The division into primitive food-gatherers and hunters, gardeners, and so on, is still assiduously supported by a number of anthropologists, especially by those who subscribe to the notion of unilinear evolution, i.e. development along a single course, in 'stages' resembling Tylor's. This has undergone some further modification – a process of further sophistication. For one thing, it pays far more attention to the social dimension and in fact accords this more or less equal weighting. The 'scale of social complexity', actually socio-political complexity, is not always spelt out *as* a scale, but it underlies a great deal of specific discussion on such topics as stateless societies, pyramidal societies, and the like. The scale, submerged or explicit, ranges from small hunting bands at one extreme to highly urbanized populations at the other. Shorn of its modern wording and detail, this double scale (economic, and socio-political) sometimes looks very much like its older counterparts. And there is a very real danger of its being handled as if it were no more than that – a somewhat creaky and sparse scaffolding embellished with modern trimmings, with no suggestion that any major structural alterations are needed. To some anthropologists, it is both a time-scale and a modernity-scale. Small, non-literate societies like those in Aboriginal Australia are described explicitly as backward, hopelessly out of date, and irrelevant. Events have passed them by. They are, says Braidwood,* on the edges of the human stage, still engrossed in the first act of a play while the rest of the world is busy with the third (the third act being Industrialization). They don't realize that the first act was over long ago and it is time to move on.

There is nothing wrong with using a framework of this kind, provided its limitations as well as its merits are clearly recognized. The problem of comparisons over a world-wide

* R. Braidwood, *Prehistoric Men*, Scott, Foresman, Glenview, Ill., 1967 (1st published by the Field Museum of Natural History), pp. 167–8.

range is a particularly intransigent one. Both uniformities and divergences need to be incorporated in any attempt at a global coverage, but the balance between the general and the particular is hard to maintain in constructing a classificatory scheme of such magnitude. One attempt to resolve the difficulties inherent in the unilinear model is Julian Steward's* 'multilinear evolutionary' approach, which makes more allowance for cultural variations and does not assume a universally constant *sequence* of stages. Other than this, however, its fundamental premises are much the same.

Differences in both economic and socio-political arrangements between societies are certainly obtrusive, and certainly lend themselves very well to scaling. Such schematic models of intersocietal comparison can be most useful for certain purposes. They make for a tidier picture, by imposing order on a mass of material, and at the same time they include enough substance to make them plausible and reasonable. But it is hard to avoid the feeling that for some social scientists it is a convenient way of dividing the human world into compartments – so that they can choose which compartments to avoid in their reading.

The current search for appropriate indexes of comparison is not confined to grosser or easily quantifiable elements, nor to the economic-socio-political fields. In that respect it is nothing new. But in earlier schemes the tendency was to subsume other features under general labels, mostly with an economic emphasis, and also to use them in more impressionistic and subjective ways, i.e. bringing them in as part of the overall model, but without specifying how they fitted in, or didn't fit in, to it. Current methods and procedures reflect the growing interest in measurement as such, and more sophisticated use of

* For example, his discussion of 'Evolution and Process', in A. L. Kroeber *et al.*, eds., *Anthropology Today*, University of Chicago Press, 1953.

statistics. There is more concern with the actual units of measurement: how they are selected, how far they are comparable if not equivalent, and so on.* In serious comparative studies, 'savage' and 'barbarian', with its 'barbarous' overtones, are no longer acceptable as labels for categories of mankind in this evolutionary type of sequence.† There is something altogether too derogatory about them, too obviously ethnocentric. When they are used now in reference to contemporary or past peoples, as they still are in some contexts, it is with this derogatory connotation – or with mock facetiousness. Their meaning lies in the contrast that is implied or inferred. They are *relative* terms, relative to some standard of behaviour or some normative assumptions about living that need not be spelt out in so many words.

In earlier evolutionary schemes and in popular usage, 'savages' were on the very bottom rung of the human scale, if they were accepted as being human at all. Purely economic considerations aside, they were regarded almost simultaneously in two, completely contradictory ways. In one, they were people with no rules except the law of the jungle: they represented the essence of lawlessness, normlessness, an extreme illustration of Hobbes's 'war of all against all'. In the other, they were rigidly bound by rules and conventions that left no room for individuality. This was, in a sense, Durkheim's

* G. Murdock's *Social Structure* (Macmillan, New York, 1949) is already to some extent outmoded in this respect. For others, see, for example, R. Naroll, *Data Quality Control. A New Research Technique*, Free Press of Glencoe, New York, 1962; and E. Bowden, 'An Index of Sociocultural Development Applicable to Precivilized Societies', *American Anthropologist*, Vol. 71, no. 3, June 1969, pp. 454–61.

† Archaeologists or archaeology-oriented anthropologists seem to have stayed with this threefold division longer than most social scientists, and to suppose that it is still generally acceptable. For example, see Glyn Daniel, *The First Civilizations. The Archaeology of their Origins*, Thames & Hudson, 1968. Also R. J. Braidwood, *Prehistoric Men*.

'solidarity of likeness', social cohesion based on uniformity, the assumption of almost complete homogeneity. A third view combined elements of both of these. The 'noble savage' of Jean-Jacques Rousseau could manage without the rules that constrained and constricted civilized man because his life was instinctively orderly and harmonious. He was 'natural man', innocent and uncorrupted, in a Garden of Eden-style setting. Anthropologists who favoured the word, for one reason or another, injected into it a much more positive meaning. Malinowski, for instance, in a kind of academic double-talk, used the label 'savages' for the Trobriand Islanders whom he put so firmly and so sympathetically on the anthropological world-map. It was as if he were saying, 'We know that this is an absolute misnomer – but the label is popularly accepted, so let's stay with it.' And perhaps he hoped to shock his readers into a reappraisal by pointing out, in effect, '*These* are your savages, these courteous and sensible people!'

But one thing common to all conventional categorizations of savages was the assumption that they were right outside the orbit of the civilized world. They might interact with one another, but that was their own affair: what they did had no real bearing on that world and posed no serious threat to it. They were outside the range of effective communication, living lives that were based on totally dissimilar premises.

In that respect, the 'barbarian' category implied something quite different. It was still contrasted with 'civilized', but the social distance between the two was seen as being less absolute. There was a dialogue between them, though an unequal one – or at least the suggestion that such a dialogue was possible, even if it was framed in military terms. In other words, they were capable of learning the rules that governed civilized man, whether or not they chose to do so. This view is perpetuated in semi-serious references to the socialization of children: the saying that every generation is faced with the influx of a fresh horde of barbarians who must be taught the right and proper way to behave because they have no understanding of such things. (The word 'savages' is sometimes substituted, in its 'no-rules' connotation.) But probably the best-known examples from European-centred history books are these two, related images: settled people, oasis and city dwellers, threatened and periodically overrun by nomadic, barbarian, Mongol hordes;* and the barbarian threats to, and final sacking of, Rome. The word 'overrun' itself suggests a disorderly, tumultuous onrush, sweeping aside all obstacles – including such obstacles as humanitarian considerations – as against the ideal (it is sometimes put in that way) of a decent, orderly, 'civilized' conquest situation, one where there is agreement on the 'rules of war' (or of peace).

This comes out particularly well in a number of accounts of the relations between Chinese civilization and the fringe people who were, from the Chinese standpoint, barbarians. One sign of the widening horizons that we spoke of before, has been a willingness on the part of Europeans to turn back on themselves the epithet 'barbarians' applied to them by others – trying to see themselves as others saw them. An entertaining example of this is Barr's† account of Japanese reactions to the intrusion of Commodore Perry and other Western barbarians.

In one particularly interesting statement from Wang Fu-chih, provided by W. T. De Bary,‡ Chinese and barba-

* For example, see *The Travels of Marco Polo*, A New Translation by R. E. Latham, The Penguin Classics (ed. by E. V. Rieu), Penguin Books, 1958, p. ix, also p. xi.

† P. Barr, *The Coming of the Barbarians, A Story of Western Settlement in Japan 1853–1870*, Macmillan, London and Melbourne, 1967.

‡ W. T. De Bary *et al.*, eds., *Sources of Chinese Tradition*, Columbia University Press, New York and London, 1960, Part Four, 'The Confucian Revival', pp. 598–603. Wang, says De Bary, was challenging the legitimacy of Manchu rule in China, since to him the Manchu were barbarians.

ians* are described as fundamentally the same but ordained by divine decree to remain separate, each in its proper place: the danger, he said, lay in the possibility of too close an association, which could be disadvantageous to both. Long before Wang's time, the T'ang empire had far-ranging contacts with 'outside' peoples. Schafer† gives a fascinating description of T'ang perspectives on these peoples and the names applied to them, such as the '*Man* Barbarians' of the south and the '*Hu* Barbarians', who included Westerners.‡ And Reischauer§ notes that, in an edict relating to the T'ang suppression of Buddhism, the Buddha himself was referred to as 'a western barbarian in origin'. He also makes the point that the monk Ennin, coming to China from a culturally-linked nation (Japan), was able to interpret what he saw and heard much more realistically than the 'barbarian' Marco Polo was able to do a few centuries later. As Reischauer says,¶ Marco Polo's reminiscences, however fascinating and wide-ranging, were just that – experiences in retrospect, a traveller's tales of mixed

* See also, for instance, R. van Gulik, *Sex and Society in Ancient China*, Brill, Leiden, 1961, pp. 10–11, 335, 336.

† E. H. Schafer, *The Golden Peaches of Samarkand. A Study of T'ang Exotics*, University of California Press, Berkeley and Los Angeles, 1963, e.g. pp. 4 and 5. Also, *The Vermilion Bird. T'ang Images of the South*, University of California Press, Berkeley and Los Angeles, 1967, e.g. pp. 53, 57, 58, 59, 70, 90, 98, 99.

‡ For some Indian perspectives on 'barbarians', notably on the 'Aryans' who flooded into the northwest of the continent, see e.g. S. Piggott, *Ancient India*. Penguin Books, 1950, pp. 144, 257–8, 260. Also, N. C. Chaudhuri, *The Continent of Circe*, Chatto & Windus, 1965, p. 57. A. L. Basham, *Studies in Indian History and Culture*. Smabodhi Pubs., Calcutta, 1964, e.g. pp. 10, 28, sees India as a land of inherent diversity, which in the past was well able to assimilate its barbarian invaders.

§ E. O. Reischauer, *Ennin's Travels in T'ang China*, The Ronald Press, New York, 1955, pp. 242–3. The Japanese Buddhist monk Ennin, visiting China, took a copy of this edict, issued in 843 by the Emperor against a Chinese Buddhist monk, Wei Tsung-ch'ing.

¶ Ibid., pp. 1, 3, 4.

accuracy, whereas Ennin's meticulously kept personal diary covers more than nine years of close, first-hand observation.

The phasing out of the words 'barbarian' and 'savage' in referring to other peoples *as* peoples, in an evolutionary model, is in line with the move toward more neutral, less emotionally charged labels in cross-cultural comparisons. In part, this reflects a more general concern with the place of values (evaluation, commitment, taking sides) in social science. Also, it reveals a growing awareness that such comparisons are not somehow isolated and separable from the 'real' world of people. They take place within a socio-cultural context which includes members of the particular societies that are the subject of study. And their response to such labels, when these are applied to themselves, has practical as well as theoretical implications.

This move, however, is still very much 'in process'. One impediment has been a stubbornly entrenched twofold dichotomy, that polarizes the major opposition in the three-fold division and omits or blurs the middle (barbarian) category. In its naïvest form it was permeated by a blatant ethnocentrism. It was a view from inside, looking out, but cloaked in the language of science – in the earlier natural history sense of science that emphasized the classifying and sorting of data. The contrast was expressed in terms of low as against high culture (or cultures), or low as against advanced society. But 'low' is almost as disparaging as 'savage', without any of the more positive qualities that *could* be attached to that word (exotic? picturesque? certainly vital). As research on the topic of social class and stratification has shown, people are not anxious to use it or have it used in reference to themselves. It is therefore out of fashion as far as such labels are concerned.

The label that supplanted it, as the polar opposite of advanced or civilized, is primitive. And this is a very stubborn label indeed. As employed by many of its supporters, it is merely a synonym for 'low', with the same range of meanings – crude, inferior, inadequate, inefficient, and so on. For others, it is a convenient shorthand label identifying a particular kind of society, at what they still think of as a particular 'stage' in the course of human development. This is, of course, the stage of hunting and food-gathering, of small bands and limited resources, simple technology, absence of writing – in short, of 'uncivilized' or 'pre-civilized' men. And a new wave of interest in contemporary small-scale societies has as its mainspring the belief that these are closer to the origins of human life, in the sense of being closer to the sub-human primates: that they represent the earliest type of man. But the neatness and apparent clarity of the word 'primitive' actually cloaks a great deal of ambiguity. And, not least, it imposes simplicity on empirical data which are actually far more complex.

As a label for any contemporary or near-contemporary group of people, 'primitive' has been under pressure, partly for this reason (vagueness, inexplicitness), partly for its invidious connotations and, again, partly because of the resentment of peoples who have been referred to in that way.* To meet these objections, some social scientists take care to specify 'inverted commas' when they use the word in this connection, but this gesture does not resolve the issue. Others have searched for labels which will point more neutrally to the criteria they use as a basis for categorizing whole societies, i.e. something more than the single items included in a comprehensive cross-cultural inventory, but less clumsy and also less redolent of the earlier economic-determinist bias attaching to 'hunters and food gatherers'.† 'Tribal' has been suggested

* See, for example, M. F. Ashley Montagu, ed., *The Concept of the Primitive*, Free Press, New York, 1968. (This includes a reprinted article by C. H. Berndt.)

† See, for example, E. R. Service, *The Hunters*, Prentice-Hall, Englewood Cliffs, N.J., 1966.

as one solution, and a number of British social anthropologists favoured it.* It suggests a certain kind of social organization, and in that sense it is reasonably acceptable, but it is far from ideal.† 'Exotic' is another label, but this has not gained general acceptance. Perhaps it sounds a little *too* glamorous. Redfield's 'folk' culture and society, small, self-contained societies that he contrasted with 'peasant' as well as with 'urban', were not the same as what he called 'primitive'.

Terms like 'pre-modern', 'pre-literate', 'pre-industrialized' savour too much of the 'outside' perspective that does not take sufficiently into account 'views from within' a particular society, its own specific ethos or themes. (It is as if labels like 'pre-television' or 'pre-colour television' were applied to some European societies. Although they are valid enough from one point of view, and helpful for survey-type comparisons, they can block or side-track other, more positive lines of analysis.) 'Non-industrialized', 'non-urbanized', 'non-literate' are much more neutral, and stipulate the specific criterion that is most salient in the approach of the speaker or writer, as being most suitable for his purpose at the time (i.e. he can change the label if he wants to focus on urbanization rather than industrialization – and so on). 'Non-literate', however, does point to a highly important feature: literacy, ability to read and to write, with all the implications of this for communication between peoples and for the development of intellectual thought. Many of the arguments summarized by

* 'Tribal' is used in odd ways, too. For example, M. McLuhan includes under 'tribal cultures' Indian and Chinese. To him, such cultures allow no scope for individual self-expression. M. McLuhan, *Understanding Media: The Extensions of Man*, Sphere Books, London, 1968 (1st pub. by Routledge and Kegan Paul, 1964), p. 94.

† As used by some writers, it is a cover for the same basic philosophy that underlies the term 'primitive'. See, e.g., M. Sahlins, *Tribesmen*, Prentice-Hall, Englewood Cliffs, N.J., 1968.

Goody* are quite pertinent, and the significance of this one aspect is incontestable.

It is true that these are negative labels: they highlight the absence of some feature, rather than the presence of something else. In fact, for some people this is what 'primitive' means – the obverse of civilized: take everything that can be subsumed under 'civilization', look for its opposite, and there you have 'primitive society', 'primitive culture'.

Herskovits, who pressed with some success for the acceptance of 'non-literate' as a replacement for 'primitive', was well aware of this disadvantage. But it was not merely that he saw it as the lesser of two evils. It *does* have wider comparative relevance – and yet it is not emotionally charged in the same sense as, say 'illiterate'. It means simply that the people so referred to have not (or did not have) a tradition or norm of literacy, and, along with this, that they have no class of specialists responsible for keeping written records. Recognizing this, Herskovits was nevertheless concerned that, in looking at such peoples, other questions too should be asked. 'What *do* they have? What positive statements can be made? What kinds of question do they themselves raise in regard to common human problems (and their own, specific, human problems) and what answers have they arrived at?' He was passionately interested in 'human rights' in the broad sense of recognition of human dignity, which, to him, meant recognition of the dignity and the special qualities of every human culture. Anthropologists have traditionally seen themselves as supporters of the 'underdog', mostly as champions of small-scale societies which seemed to be in danger of losing their cultural integrity. (There are exceptions, of course. Not all anthropologists take this line, and some go contrary to it.)

* J. Goody and I. Watt, in J. Goody, ed., *Literacy in Traditional Societies*, Cambridge University Press, 1968 (actually published in 1969), e.g. p. 49.

Herskovits' theory of cultural relativism* was a very distant relative of Karl Mannheim's sociology of knowledge (with its theme of social 'relationism', the crucial importance of 'where one stands' in the social hierarchy as a determining factor in social action and social comment). The actual mechanics as well as the conceptual underpinning of the cultural relativism approach presented enormous difficulties, and Herskovits came under heavy fire from all sides – philosophers, anthropologists, and social scientists generally. But the fundamental lesson that he tried to impart – and it *was* an attempt in this direction, a crusade as much as an academic exercise – has had a more lasting impact. In saying this, we do recognize the difficulty here. It is hard enough to measure the effects of even one of the mass media, for instance (e.g. television), and to separate out sources of influence or cause-and-effect relations. But 'the Herskovits line' in this respect certainly anticipated, and now coincides with, a climate of world opinion in which the essence of what he advocated is taken very much more for granted.

Of course, he was not the first nor the only exponent of that line. It was, and is, inherent in any investigation into a people's own socio-cultural categories of belief and action. Its immediate anthropological ancestors and contemporaries in North America were Franz Boas and Edward Sapir, as well as Ruth Benedict (her *Patterns of Culture* is a classic now, controversial but provocative). To A. L. Kroeber† this principle was a long-standing one in Anthropology – although the search for universal or even absolute values was, to him, of even greater importance. Benjamin Whorf's investigation of

* See, for example, M. Herskovits, *Man and his Works*, Knopf, New York, 1949 (1st pub. 1947), Chapter 5; also, his subsequent statement, not long before his death: 'Some Further Comments on Cultural Relativism', *American Anthropologist*, Vol. 60, No. 2 (Part 1), 1958, pp. 266–73.

† *The Nature of Culture* (collected papers), University of Chicago Press, 1952, p. 6.

linguistic categories among North American Indians, specifically among the Hopi, inspired by Sapir's earlier work, had exciting theoretical implications. It stimulated a tremendous new awareness of the place of language in culture. In particular, it underlined the far from haphazard interconnections between 'thought patterns' and language in any given society – and the corresponding disjunctions *between* societies, or between distinct speech communities.* The moral in all this was that the old warning of *traduttore, traditore* applied not simply to linguistic features alone, but to socio-cultural features in general: that the categories of one language, or of one society or culture, should not be imposed on another. And this is exactly what Herskovits, too, was saying. In the linguistic field, the two trains of inquiry that have led out from it are semantics (inquiry into meaning, in the broadest sense) on one hand, and the increasingly precise and exact study now known as structural linguistics, virtually a discipline in itself. And another point is also relevant to us here. The reports of these investigations challenged earlier assumptions about the 'primitive', 'savage', 'barbarous' languages of small-scale societies. They contended that there was no such thing as a primitive as against a civilized language, and their findings have been supported by subsequent research. (Predominantly linguistic references would be out of place here, but many general anthropological texts contain brief accounts of language and communication.)†

A corollary of this increasingly more sensitive appreciation of human socio-cultural diversity is an equally sensitive

* For a useful overview of this, see H. Hoijer, ed., *Language in Culture* (American Anthropological Association, Volume 56, No. 6, Part 2, Memoir No. 79), Chicago University Press, 1954.

† See, for example, R. L. Beals and H. Hoijer, *An Introduction to Anthropology*, Macmillan, New York, 1956, Chapter 17; J. Honigmann, *The World of Man*, Harper & Bros., New York, 1959, Chapter 32.

appreciation of human similarities: of the essential unity of mankind as such, the fact that all living peoples belong to the species known as 'modern man' or, more precisely (but also, in some eyes, more ironically), as *homo sapiens*.

In modern Anthropology this unity is accepted as a basic premise. Earlier it was not – in part, no doubt, as a consequence of the 'culture shock' experienced by people coming into contact for the first time with strikingly divergent ways of life. The gulf between primitive and civilized was envisaged as almost, though not quite, unbridgeable: as a cleavage, not simply in degree, but in kind. Now, however, even those anthropologists who refuse to jettison the word 'primitive' mostly make it plain that they see this as a division or series of divisions *within* humanity, not a division between 'human' and something else.* In that framework it may not be saying much more than is covered in popular phrases about the 'veneer of civilization', 'scratch a civilized man and you'll find a savage', and so on. But archaeologists as well as anthropologists have taken pains to stipulate that 'there is no such thing as primitive man, only primitive culture' (or society), and, a pertinent reminder, 'not everyone living within a civilization can automatically be defined as civilized'. And most anthropologists, however much they might differ on other points, would probably agree that 'civilization' is not something unique and unprecedented but a special manifestation of culture – culture in the anthropological, 'way of life', sense, that is an attribute of every human society.

We have been talking about various categories that have

* Even a publisher's comment on a series called 'Foundations of Modern Anthropology', which helps to perpetuate an outmoded stereotype of Anthropology in noting that 'It is concerned mainly with exotic peoples, prehistoric times, unwritten languages, and unlikely customs', nevertheless underlines the common-humanity aspect (Prentice-Hall International Inc., 1970 'Sociology and Anthropology' Catalogue, p. 24).

been proposed as a basis for assessing differences and similarities among the world's peoples, and the labels that have been attached to them. The 'constant' in these formally distinct categories has been the word 'civilization' or its equivalents. But what *is* civilization?

3

– And Civilization

IF some commercial advertisements are to be believed, the major determinant of civilization is material equipment – the *right* material equipment. 'Civilized living can be yours' if you purchase a particular kind of house in a particular suburb, or acquire a 'civilized car'. If the advertisers were asked what they meant, they would probably reply that their readers would know. And they could well be right.

Without attempting a systematic survey or thinking about sampling, it can be an interesting exercise to ask a fairly wide range of friends, relatives and neighbours what they understand by the word 'civilization'. The replies are likely to fall into two roughly defined categories with an area of overlap – as most statements about 'civilization' do.

The most important thing to some people is the material aspect; they emphasize visible, tangible and technical achievements: food production, domestication of animals, metallurgy, occupational specialization, the codification of laws in a formalized system of social control, and, perhaps above all, writing and the establishment of cities.* (Architecture is sub-

* For example, G. Childe, ibid., p. 31; R. J. Braidwood, *Prehistoric Men*, pp. 88, 136–9. R. E. Latham, in his Introduction to the 1958 Penguin edition of *The Travels of Marco Polo* (p. xx), draws attention to Marco Polo's use of *domesce*, as the nearest equivalent to the idea of 'civilization' but with a 'mercantile' flavour, and also to his 'chivalrous' reference to Tartars.

sumed under this last point. But the graphic and plastic arts are not drawn upon in making such assessments. One can have barbaric splendour, apparently, and art developments that are both vigorous and elegantly sophisticated, without qualifying for admission into the civilized world.)

Other writers emphasize intangibles, including moral and aesthetic qualities but virtually always in conjunction with the same material bases. Where there is elaboration on either or both aspects, tangible and intangible, it was once fashionable to speak of high, higher or advanced civilizations. (Kroeber favoured these labels, but he also spoke of 'heightening' civilizations.) They are now usually called, more neutrally, complex civilizations.

Robert Redfield in particular, is often mentioned as an exponent of the view that civilization ideally involves a growing concern with *humanity* and *humaneness* – respect for other people as persons, and reluctance to injure or destroy them.* In this he followed, among others, Kroeber, but in a less obviously 'unilinear evolutionary' framework. He was optimistic about the future of mankind on this score of moral progress, just as Kroeber and Tylor† and so many others had been. However gloomy the prospect might seem at times, he believed that things were gradually getting better.

As far as aesthetic considerations are concerned, these impinge on the 'social relations' aspect, but only partly so. They are associated just as conspicuously with the 'material' dimension. Politeness, elegance, urbanity, civility, are some-times taken as *the* criterion of civilized living, implying a certain kind of behaviour toward other people, but implying also a certain level of material comfort.‡ (Hence the mixed

* He affirms this belief in *The Primitive World and its Transformations*, Cornell University Press, 1953.

† *Anthropology*, pp. 24, 438–40.

‡ Chad Oliver gives a fictional account of a pseudo-primitive

appeal of such advertisements as those we have cited – an appeal drawing on both aspects.) But social scientists reacting against the materialistic-economic criterion as a *sine qua non* and against the 'savage' (etc.) stereotype, have deliberately applied the label 'civilization' to small-scale non-literate societies which had their own kinds of complexity and their own codes of politeness but lacked most or all of the other features usually stipulated as essential to this. (Lloyd Warner, for instance, gave his study of Australian Aborigines in north-central Arnhem Land the title *A Black Civilization.**)

There is also another side to the emphasis on intangible aspects in defining civilization. For this, we can turn to Bierstedt.† Acknowledging with regret that the rule of law is no longer adequate as an 'objective criterion' that could 'serve as an index of civilization', he proposed another: 'a literate sophistication' involving 'self-reflection and self-criticism and other-awareness' which, he says, an 'uncivilized society' does not have. Along with this goes the index of 'sociology', the sophisticated recognition of similarity-underlying-diversity in

___

society which has, so to speak, gone *beyond* the material paraphernalia that cluttered its development, in order to live more simply: 'Rite of Passage', in *Another Kind*, Ballantine Books, New York, 1955. This is rather like the 'sophisticated primitivism' that R. H. Brewer and C. E. Miner speak of (in *Japanese Court Poetry*, The Cresset Press, London, 1962, p. 89), where urban poets attempt to recapture the simplicity of an earlier and rustic style, but do so in their own more sophisticated fashion. The field of 'modern' or 'contemporary' art offers numerous examples of the same trend.

* New York, Harper, 1937/1958. A. Métraux speaks of Easter Island culture as a 'Stone Age civilization'. (*Easter Island: A Stone Age Civilization of the Pacific*, in a translation by M. Bullock, Oxford University Press, 1957.) But the rationale here is not the same, because he could draw on one conventionally accepted criterion – a written script.

† 'Indices of Civilization', *The American Journal of Sociology*, Vol. LXXI, No. 5, 1966, p. 490; also Pitrim Sorokin's 'Comments . . .' ibid., pp. 491–2.

human societies. His 'primitive', 'uncivilized' society seems to be more than a conceptual opposite to a civilized society, although his characterization of it has a non-empirical, polemical ring: it 'has art but no aesthetics, religion but no theology, techniques but no science, tools but no technology, legends but no literature, a language but no alphabet (or ideographs), customs but no laws, a history but no historiography, knowledge but no epistemology, and finally a *Weltanschauung* but no philosophy'. As he puts it, this is a direct either-or plus-or-minus polarization, with no apparent room for intermediate gradations.

And, still on the matter of 'something more than material factors', but remembering that for the majority of writers on this topic the material aspect (cities, writing, technology) is crucial, in a number of discussions of 'What is civilization?' the kind of optimism or forward-looking orientation that Redfield and others have shown, is implied as being almost a criterion in itself. This is especially likely when it is translated into a programme of vigorous action – an aggressive, outward-looking, thrusting approach to other peoples, but one still somehow combined with the criterion of disciplined self-restraint and a feeling for 'law and order'. Toynbee* saw this as a process of 'challenge and response' – but, clearly, as a two-way phenomenon: response to a challenge and also provision of a challenge: what Kroeber† called the 'cutting edge' of civilization. Small-scale non-literate societies might be bellicose, but they were not bellicose enough: they lacked both incentive and means.

* A. Toynbee, e.g. in *Civilization on Trial*, Geoffrey Cumberledge, Oxford University Press, 1946/53, p. 12. In keeping with this, he also (pp. 8–9) spoke of civilization as an 'enterprise'.

† 'The Ancient Oikumene as a Historic Culture Aggregate', The Huxley Memorial Lecture for 1945, reprinted in *The Nature of Culture*, Chicago University Press, 1952, p. 381.

By the same token, the argument would apply to a society that was very different indeed: the exquisitely polished Heian culture of Japan, focused on Kyoto, that reached its zenith in the tenth century A.D. and comes to life for the non-specialist reader in Arthur Waley's translation of Lady Murasaki's novel, *The Tale of Genji*,* and the little *Pillow Book of Sei Shonagon*.† The reader is absorbed so sympathetically into this highly structured, court-centred society that it comes as something of a shock to realize, from Ivan Morris's‡ account of the period in *The World of the Shining Prince*, just how small a space it covered and how closed it actually was. Cut off from mainland China by the collapse of T'ang, it cherished the Chinese language and classics as survivals from a bygone era§ much as educated Europe looked back to Greece, or Rome. In so doing, it gave this foreign segment of its own heritage a distinctive setting. For all that it owed to other sources, Heian civilization had its own special flavour, a combination of qualities unique to itself. Nevertheless, it was what Kenneth Clarke would label a static society. After a long phase of borrowing from outside, mainly from China, it was in a phase almost of retreat. Lacking enough stimulation in outside contacts to keep it viable, it carried within itself, as Morris shows, the seeds of its own downfall.

This brings us back to the subject of contact between societies – diffusion and innovation, people moving outside their own socio-cultural boundaries, and situations that

---

* First published by Allen and Unwin in 6 volumes, 1925–33. (One-volume edition, 1953.) See also A. S. Omori and K. Doi, trans., *Diaries of Court Ladies of Old Japan*, Kenkyusha Ltd., Tokyo, 1963 (1st published 1935).

† Unwin Books, 1960 (1st published 1928).

‡ Penguin Books, 1969 (a Peregrine Book). (First published 1964.) He includes a useful summary (Appendix 2, pp. 301–5) of the state of 'civilization' in other parts of the world at that time.

§ ibid., pp. 23–5, 28, 32.

favour the exchange of goods and ideas. Up to a point, this is the old 'cross-roads' idea. 'Roads' are a basic feature of it – land and sea routes, ranging from the well defined but less visible tracks along which goods travelled from one group to another in Aboriginal Australia, to great caravan routes like the Silk Road and the Tartary Road of central Asia. (M. Beurdeley, in *Porcelain of the East India Companies,** suggests that one reason for the weakening of the Roman Empire was its 'costly luxury trade' with countries like China. W. Willetts' *Foundations o, Chinese Art*† is another fascinating account of 'borrowing' and diffusion in this broad region.) But such paths are not enough in themselves. The crucial aspect is *cross*-roads, places at which people coming from different points can meet more or less regularly over a fairly long period.

If the contrast or clash is too extreme, however, communication is impeded. A parallel can be drawn here with raiding and war. These can be vehicles for transmission of goods and ideas; but overwhelming devastation can have, at least temporarily, the opposite effect.

Another example is what anthropologists call 'culture shock'. Many of us still regard this as a necessary initiation rite for anyone wanting to enter the profession. Whatever society he chooses to specialize in later, including his own, an anthropologist's first field research experience should bring him into close contact with a system of values so unlike his own that it gives him a mental and emotional jolt: it should force him to take a new look at assumptions that he formerly regarded as natural and inevitable. This does not mean that he rejects those assumptions, but it does mean that he is more aware of them, that he no longer takes them for granted but recognizes that there are *legitimate* alternatives. (Herskovits' cultural relativism again: not just an acknowledgement that some societies are

* Barrie & Rockcliff, 1962.
† Thames & Hudson, 1965 ed.

grounded in different premises, but an acknowledgement also that it is quite natural for them to be so, that they have a right to live in accordance with their own values. We shall return to this contention later.) Too much in the way of 'culture shock', however, and the anthropologist (or whoever it is) goes home, or tries to go home – retreats, back to familiar territory. Too little, and the contrast lacks sharpness: no shock, no jolt into a new awareness. But this is not the place to take up the question of 'how much is too much', or 'too little'. Even in the matter of anthropological field experience alone, persons and circumstances vary considerably, and to discuss this adequately would mean bringing in far too much detail.

When it came to looking at the exotic world outside Europe, the continent of Africa was one region that caught the imagination of anthropologists as well as others – not merely administrators and politicians, missionaries, traders, and so on, but also people who read about it or visited it for pleasure and interest rather than utility. Even though so much still remains unrecorded, it was richly documented in comparison with many other areas. Not least, it included 'pre-industrial' cities, as among the Yoruba, kingdoms like the Nupe, formal paraphernalia of established authority – chiefs, 'kings', 'priests', officers and ranks to which Europeans could attach familiar terms. Although alien, here was something that Europeans could grasp. Even more 'tribal' people like the Nuer were reasonably intelligible to them. From an outsider's point of view, this was partly perhaps because they belonged within the wider African framework in which organized states were so prominent, partly because they too shared in the cattle-complex and were not hunters and food-collectors like the Kalahari Bushmen, and partly because their pride, self-confidence and politico-military aggressiveness forced an assessment of them in something resembling their own terms.

Not all 'tribal' people had this advantage. Marginal peoples, small-scale societies, without cattle, without a wealth of material equipment, were much more vulnerable. And they were away from the main cross-roads – as Africa, directly in its coastal regions, indirectly farther inland, was not. Their weakness in the face of superior war-making machinery and political strategy was obvious; but, over and above immediate defence-implications, it had long-range consequences. For one thing, outsiders had fewer incentives to try to understand them – blinded by the conviction, often put more or less in these words, that there was nothing to understand. Settled, war-conscious people like the New Zealand Maoris fared rather better, if only because these two features (settled dwellings and organized warfare) were familiar, culturally congenial, to Europeans. Others, like the Australian Aborigines, came off badly. It was hard for Europeans, even interested Europeans, to get inside their skin.

But why have various societies taken shape along certain lines rather than others? This is one of the most intriguing questions that can be asked about human socio-cultural development. It is also one to which there are as yet no satisfactory answers – only plenty of tentative suggestions, although some of them purport to be more than that. Crossroads, busy or otherwise, can be a source of cultural differentiation, but so can isolation. A 'basic invention', as Linton (and others) have suggested, can lead to further inventions* in the same direction. Two popular illustrations are, of course, the invention of fire, and the invention of the wheel – in the mechanical, not the symbolic (Buddhist Wheel of Life) sense, although that could have ramifications in other ways.

* R. Linton, *The Study of Man. An Introduction*, Appleton-Century, 1936, pp. 316–17 (in Chapter XVIII, 'Discovery and Invention'). See also R. L. Rands and C. Riley, 'Diffusion and Discontinuous Distribution', *American Anthropologist*, 60, 2, Part I, 1958, pp. 274–97, esp. p. 277.

Among anthropologists, Kroeber combined careful documenting of concrete detail with a macroscopic, 'wide sweep' approach to cultural patterns and cultural change on a global basis. Cultural themes, stimulus diffusion, the importance of cultural style, cultural intensity, direction, and 'divertibility' were among the important features he drew upon in explaining variation and stability, acceptance and negation, in specific instances and in larger perspective. In many respects his overall perspective resembled Toynbee's, especially when he was asking much the same questions about the rise and fall of civilizations. But he was critical of Toynbee, just as he was critical of archaeologists like Gordon Childe, who appeared to him to be neglecting the relation between technological developments and the totality of culture. Toynbee, in turn, has been accused of failing 'to understand the archaeological record'.* The answers suggested by archaeologists and prehistorians are part of the larger 'historical' answer, where the main framework consists of a sequence of events through time. Answers along these lines, of course, do not exclude 'sociological'-type answers: the two are not, or need not be, mutually opposed. But 'how' questions are much simpler to answer than 'why' questions: how a society changes, how such-and-such an item is accepted or rejected. And so on.

We shall come back later to some of these broader issues.

Now, however, we turn to two societies of the kind that Toynbee (though not Kroeber) dismissed from consideration, in his broad schema, as the 'outer proletariat', societies of no consequence in the course of world affairs. We can do no more than glance at them – or some facets of them. In both respects we have had to be selective. But the choice is not quite fortuitous. In the first place, they represent two regions that are of considerable interest in the light of what we have

* G. Daniel, *The Idea of Prehistory*, Watts, 1962, 141–2; also, *The First Civilizations. The Archaeology of their Origins*, pp. 16–17.

been talking about. The Aborigines of Australia have long been a favourite in the 'Foot-of-the-human-ladder-Stakes': in some accounts they are rated as being the most primitive of all. The New Guinea peoples are rated a little higher, as 'settled horticulturists', but still well within the old category of 'savages'. In the second place, these are regions in which we ourselves have carried out first-hand field research, so that the details of our discussion do not rest on information from other people.

The points we want to demonstrate, however, could have been made in relation to almost any non-literate society, chosen at random. The anthropological literature provides a wealth of material, more substantial than travellers' tales, that attempts to look at such societies (and others) not only from the outside, but also from the standpoint of the people within them.

PART 2

PEOPLE 'OUTSIDE'

4

In Aboriginal Australia

POPULAR misconceptions of Australian Aborigines used to be almost identical with stereotypes of 'savages' – because to many people that was just what they were. In the 'noble savage' view they were paragons of virtue, unselfishly sharing all they had, submerging the individual in the community – 'primitive communism'. In the 'no-rules' view, they were savages of the most bestial sort, without graces or redeeming features, barely human. In a third, they were (and are) living representatives of the Old Stone Age: in effect, 'this is what people, or almost-people, must have been like in those days'.

This view is very controversial indeed. It has implications for the scientific investigations of human beginnings, of course. But it is all too easy to single out one material or economic trait (use of stone axes; hunting and gathering techniques) and highlight it at the expense of intangibles – and to brush aside the long centuries of development in which human cultures

43

have proceeded along different lines, with their own particular emphases. The assumption that a European-centred classification of stone-tool sequences, for example, could be superimposed neatly on other parts of the world, including Australia, has only recently been shaken. Discovery of such material as polished stone hand axes in western Arnhem Land, which appear to date from a period before such artifacts were being made in Europe, is among the new evidence that is helping archaeologists to fit together a new mosaic of ideas about the Aboriginal past. But this is only one facet, and one that must be related to other aspects of Aboriginal living. And there remains the broad methodological issue of categorizing and comparing peoples, or cultures, over the entire spectrum of their respective 'ways of life'.

For most of southern Australia, we have no details of Aboriginal culture as a going concern, only a patchy and incomplete record. It was hard for outsiders, and especially for European outsiders to get close enough to Aborigines, physically or otherwise, even to begin to see them in their own terms. Mutual ignorance was the rule, even in circumstances where some working consensus seemed to have been reached. Linguistic misunderstandings were only the tip of the iceberg. Apart from the most obvious features (e.g. the Europeans' abundance of material goods, the Aborigines' lack of them), there was almost total miscomprehension of each other's way of life.

The Aborigines responded with psychological withdrawal and reticence and physical dependence, punctuated with aggression. They hardly attempted to bridge the gap by articulating their socio-cultural background to people who appeared to be operating on completely different premises. To make matters worse, they were politically weak. They were not organized for offence or defence except on a very localized and sporadic basis, and then never to protect their territories. To them, the land was god-given, never a prize to be won or lost. They were hopelessly ill-equipped to cope with a large-scale invasion.

The Europeans, for their part, saw the Aborigines through a negative screen, focused on what they did not have or did not do, or what they 'did wrong'. The outcome in print was almost a foregone conclusion: they fitted convincingly into the framework of primitive, savage, if not barbarous man – because that was the framework imposed on them. There was just enough substance in the more serious and sympathetic reports, and just enough vocabulary, to intrigue 'armchair scholars' overseas, and a certain amount of individual-experience evidence to demonstrate that Aborigines were really human, after all. But the overall picture was one of *minimal* humanity. The outcome of this negative view as far as practical welfare went, also seemed to be inevitable. But that is another story.

It is amazing that earlier investigators were able to record as much about Aboriginal life as they did – men such as Baldwin Spencer and his sometime collaborator F. Gillen, and missionaries like Carl Strehlow. Systematic research was only beginning then, and as procedures and techniques improved, traditional Aboriginal customs were changing too. But enough of them remained, notably in sparsely settled areas and reserves in the centre and north, to indicate how *lacking* in crudity Aboriginal life must have been throughout the continent, despite its very conspicuous material disadvantages. It is true that, in every Aboriginal group, social relations rested on the premise that interdependence was crucial to survival. This was 'community through necessity', community feeling dictated much more obviously by environmental circumstance than in many other human societies. Rights and duties were fairly tightly defined, mainly on the basis of kinship and other social relationships. But along with these went rules of etiquette that helped to define the *quality* of those relationships.

Although they were quarrelsome enough in some circumstances, in camp fights and revenge expeditions and sorcery accusations, the Aborigines were on the whole a polite people. Their rules of politeness varied between one tribe and another, like their views on what constituted good behaviour and what did not. But they had a substantial amount in common. Also, though this was less apparent because of cultural differences, they had a substantial amount in common with polite Europeans: fundamentally, in terms of acting with due regard for other people's feelings and wishes, and formally in terms of such things as etiquette in speech (courteous as against blunt ways of making a request), in sharing food and in exchanging gifts, or sitting circumspectly (an important point, for people with no clothing and a minimum of body coverings). And so on. In fact, this meant no more than behaving as a normal, responsible human person in contrast to uncouth, non-human beings like malignant spirits – or other Aborigines known only through hearsay and not through direct contact.

In areas where detailed research into traditional life has been possible, the picture that has been emerging is utterly unlike the earlier sketches of a rough and savage people. Their religious and mundane affairs are coherent and sophisticated. And, in both, what we could call 'surface' images as well as less obvious symbolic allusions are almost commonplace.

The culture of Western Desert Aborigines, for example, might seem to be quite simple, almost elemental, but this appearance is deceptive. It is a surface simplicity. Their verbal culture, their traditional word-patterning, can be viewed on two levels – or rather on two *main* levels: other lines of analysis are possible within these. At one level there is the straightforward, almost photographic realism of their references to the natural environment. They reproduce faithfully and perceptively its most significant features, from weather phenomena (changing cloud shapes and colours, differences in volume and sound of rainfall, etc.) to topography. The other is the level of symbolic statement, the equivalent of geometric or non-representational art, as in the stylized ground-designs of these Desert areas. Their meaning is not 'given'. It cannot be understood from the ordinary word-pictures alone.

The same twofold distinction could be drawn throughout Aboriginal Australia, with varying degrees of complexity. It does not coincide with the division some earlier writers tried to make. In reporting on Aboriginal culture, they identified men with all that was sacred, knowing all the esoteric details and symbolism, and women as profane (or mundane), confined to a shallower, superficial involvement. Later investigations have shown that this was a false picture. Aboriginal men had a deeper and wider knowledge of symbolic allusions, since they were responsible for controlling and organizing virtually all of the most important religious affairs. But this is a contrast *within* the realm of symbolic interpretations, not between that realm and something else.

Another point, in regard to levels of complexity, relates to the 'musical' aspect of Aboriginal songs. Sophisticated ethnomusicological research on these is very recent indeed, but enough has already been done to demonstrate *their* sophistication. In this respect, as well as in their word-content, the songs are both varied and intricate. In northern South Australia, work in the late 1960s (by Dr Catherine Ellis, of the University of Adelaide) has shown that adults introduce children first to a deliberately simplified melodic song-structure, and gradually and consistently elaborate on it.

It is impossible to do justice to Aboriginal symbolic interpretations in a short discussion even if we confine it (as we shall do here) to words alone without bringing in graphic and plastic arts. This is a problem of presentation. In a way, it is like the problem facing a person who is trying to tell a rather obscure joke. People who share the same background of experience are likely to appreciate it. Others need a lengthy explanation, that they may not have the incentive or the patience to follow.

In the Aboriginal case, the most straightforward descriptive statements need little more than a few comments on their setting and their meaning. Word-images of trees, flowers and other natural phenomena can be transmitted directly across cultural boundaries: for instance, this summary of a rain-magic sequence* from the Canning Stock Route in the Western Desert of Western Australia. In its aim, it is a magical formula. But in its choice of words, as well as in its rather catchy rhythm and melody, it becomes much more than that.

The word-pictures in each short song are cumulative, leading up to the hoped-for result. Clouds of varying shapes and sizes appear on the horizon, rising massively. The earth below them grows warmer and more humid. A little bird, associated with water and waterholes, hops about expectantly. Lightning plays in the sky, and a strong wind breaks branches from the trees. The first rain drops patter lightly on the ground. At last the clouds stand directly overhead and rain pours down with the heavy sound of thunder, while water, trickling at first, goes running in all directions – streams flowing, rock-holes filling; even the smallest soaks [points where water can be obtained by digging, e.g. in dry sandy creek-beds] are renewed and revived.

In other examples, it is the human relations in a song or story that come through most clearly. The sweetheart-theme in western Arnhem Land 'gossip songs' is usually treated quite simply. We use the word 'gossip' because they are composed by contemporary songmen on the basis of overheard conversations and gossip – although, perhaps to evade responsibility for what he has to say, the understanding is that the songman merely repeats songs given to him in dreams by his personal

* See C. H. Berndt, 'The Arts of Life. An Australian Aboriginal Perspective', *Westerly*, Vol. 1, Nos. 2 and 3, 1962, p. 83. A professional geographer reported that the sequence corresponds exactly with the normal regional pattern of first rains after a drought.

spirit familiar (e.g. a frog, a lizard, a Rainbow snake, or the ghost of a child). Some bring in more subtle play on words, mainly by way of *double entendre*. Others, stimulatory in intent, are bluntly erotic. Often they take the form of soliloquies, or conversations between two or three people, one of them sighing for an absent lover. 'Look, this is where the two of us were sitting together, only yesterday!' 'Look at that fire burning, far away. Do you suppose *she* lit it, thinking of me?' 'My eyes are wet with tears. When will he return?' And so on.

The characters are always unnamed and the incidents unlocated. For people who listen to the songs and afterwards talk about them and sing them to themselves, they are a kind of informal guessing game. The songman himself always knows who triggered off each song, but usually doesn't tell, and the wording is vague enough to encourage speculation. Without going into this matter of identification, here are two very short examples. Both are in the Gunwinggu language, and the vernacular is given in footnotes.

In the first,* a man (or a woman) is sad because his sweetheart is going away.

> Today (s)he's leaving, today (s)he's leaving –
>> Oh, it's no good!
> (S)he could have stayed one more (day)!
>> Oh, what shall I do?

In the second,† a man worries because his sweetheart seems

---

*   Bólgimi gárei, bólgimi gárei –
                    Gaménmenwari!
                Nug gúngudji níwerin!
                    Bálei nug ngaiimi?
(*Bólgimi* is 'today' or 'now'.)

†   Gagébbumi ngádug –
                    Nyáleigen gagebbúmi?
                Bólgimi ngámwam ngánang –
                    Yibékkaii ngádug?

cross with him, and asks a go-between to find out what is the matter.

> Her face is sulky, my own one –
>> *Why* is her face sulky?
> Today I came, and I saw her –
>> Would you find out about it,* for me?

All of these were, traditionally, destined to be transient, sung and remembered only until they were superseded by new songs composed along much the same lines. In this they differed, not only from sacred myth-songs, but also from the children's songs which used to be common in western Arnhem Land. These were bright little snippets of song, varying in tune, about the birds, fish, plants and other things in their natural environment; they were not 'composed', but handed on from one generation to another.

Not all of the gossip songs are about sweethearts. Small items of personal experience, which need not exclude experiences of the songman himself, are enough to start a song. This example† is one of the shortest of all. (When it was in vogue, in the early 1950s, people gave three different identifications for it, all very positively, apart from the songman's.) Someone joining a group of people is abashed when they all look at her (or him).

> Now that I've come,‡ you all look at me –
> All of you, eyes looking at me!

In the gossip songs also, people weep for their home country, gazing toward it, longing to be there. This 'feeling

* 'Would you listen for me?' Or, 'Would you listen to my own one?' (*Ngadug*, 'mine' or 'for me', is also a term of endearment.) It is not 'Would you ask?' but more like, 'Would you sound her out for me?'
†   Bólgimi ngámwam, ngándinan –
                    Gúnmim róg ngandináni!
‡ Or, 'Today I came . . .'

for home' is something that permeates Aboriginal myth and song, but it is a sentiment that others too, not Aborigines, can share and appreciate. And the songs and chants that convey a sharper grief have a much wider human relevance. A lament for a loved spouse or a dead child, although couched in a particular local idiom, is universally intelligible in its emotion.

Beyond this more readily translatable level, however, communication becomes increasingly difficult without – and even with – a fair amount of specific annotation. The reason is, of course, that this 'deeper' level is much more closely tied to its socio-cultural context. To be at all adequate, any account of meaning at that level must include some reference to that context, and the more foreign it is felt to be, the harder it is to find a bridge of meaning. In Aboriginal Australia, the verbal and visual arts are closely intermeshed with the social dimension, with all its complexities: the social units and categories, including kinship, that outsiders seem to find especially alien and especially irrelevant to modern living. In consequence, there is a tendency to avoid dwelling on this dimension in talking about Aboriginal poetic language, except in a more detailed treatise. And this means that the intricacies of that language are all too easily overlooked or ignored.

Take, for instance, one area: north-eastern Arnhem Land, on the tropical northern coast facing the Arafura Sea. It would be easy to provide a colourful account of the imagery in their myths and songs, without going any deeper into the question of 'meaning' to the people themselves. All the creatures and plants and places that are important to them are mentioned in some way in these songs: anything that 'has a name', however small. And they are linked and cross-linked in a variety of combinations of interlocking symbols. At one level, then, we can simply enjoy the word-pictures. Coconuts and empty canoes and seed pods from unidentified trees come tossing and splashing on the waves, pushed by the north-east wind at the end of the wet season. The morning star shines on the sea, and on the islands and mainland. The current swirls and splashes around a sacred rock out in the sea, 'singing' to itself. Crocodiles sleep in soft mud by the mangroves where sandflies dance, and when the tide is far out the mud flats are absolutely still, with no stirring of air or wind. Away inland, eucalypt trees bend over a clear pool, with bees and various birds dancing around their white blossoms, searching for honey, until the petals drift to the ground and over the surface of the water. The soft hands of the rain touch the earth lightly, bringing new shoots to life, with heavier falls coming behind. A seagull walks alone on a flat beach at low tide. A 'Macassan' prau moves westward along the coast, sails flapping and mast dipping in the wind, while local spirits watch it from the shore, wailing farewell.

The difficulty, in drawing attention to such images, is to know when and where to stop. Still at this surface level, there are the different, slightly overlapping, approaches taken by various songs to the same natural phenomenon. The 'red sky at sunset' appears in a number of quite different songs, usually as the concluding image in a sequence, but the sequences themselves are distinct. Wind and rain are named according to the directions from which they come, and each has its own song-cycles. With them go differing cloud-formations, in characteristic shapes and colours, and these again are traced to a variety of origins – spray from a whale or dugong, the cloud-white hands of spirit women mixing cycad-palm 'flour', smoke from a fire.

But at this point, evading for the moment the specific symbolic meanings of such images, we can hardly talk about variation without bringing in the social dimension. The absolute minimum necessary for understanding it, is this.

In relations between individual persons, the most fundamental guide to behaviour between them is kinship, ranging from actual blood-relationships within the immediate family, to distant or nominal ties with people who are almost, but not quite, strangers. Cutting across these are several other divisions. One is categorization into moieties ('halves'). All of north-eastern Arnhem Land, the entire human and natural world, is divided into two moieties, *dua* and *jiridja* (yiridja). Every person belongs to one or the other, on the basis of patrilineal descent (i.e. membership comes down through the male line), and one strictly observed marriage rule is that husband and wife should always be of opposite moieties: a *dua* person must marry a *jiridja* person. (There are other marriage rules, too.) Then there are several kinds of social unit that belong to one moiety or the other, never to both. The two most important are the *mada*, which literally means 'tongue' – a dialect unit; and *mala*, which we translate as 'clan'. They also are based on patrilineal descent, and exist in paired combinations: every person belongs to one *mada-mala* pair. To simplify this dis-cussion, let us ignore the *mala* and just think of the *mada*.

The two moieties are, conventially, contrasting and comple-mentary, not only in regard to marriage but also in the sharing of myths and songs, and collaboration in ritual. For example, most of the material on contact with the outside world – Indonesians ('Macassans'), Japanese and Europeans – is en-shrined in traditions of the *jiridja* moiety. Among the word-images we listed, the crocodile-mangrove complex and the coconuts and cycad palm and the Macassan prau are *jiridja*, the seagull (that particular one) is *dua* and so is the sequence that includes the eucalypts by the pool. Clouds and rain are divided between the two. For example, the north-west monsoon is *dua*, like the 'honey wind' from the south. Fire, actually 'bush fire', belongs to both moieties, but their song-sequences are quite distinct in patterning although the images are similar. Both deal with the huge fires that can sweep across the inland in the dry season, like the seasonal burning-off and

hunting fires that are set in train by ordinary people, but in
this case possibly started by (for example) lightning strikes.
In both sequences the most vigorous singing depicts the noise,
wind, billowing smoke and huge sheets of flame at the height
of the blaze, and their ferocious speed. They soften dramatically to dwell on the little flickering, smouldering remnants
when everything around is charred and blackened. And they
conclude with the red sky of sunset. In between, they detail
the kinds of grass and trees that are affected – and the places
where all of this happens.

This last point is important. The whole countryside is
apportioned out among the various *mada-mala* pairs. The actual
boundary lines between them are not really crucial. What
matters is that they represent constellations of named sites,
some of them highly sacred and secret, and some noted for the
foods available there at appropriate seasons.

The songs belong to specific *mada* within the overall moiety
framework. The '*dua* fire' sequence is shared among a number
of *dua* moiety *mada*, but they use rather different words and a
different singing style: Riradjingu *mada* style is not the same
as Djambarbingu, for instance, or Djabu.

The songs differentiate between *mada* territories, in drawing
attention to sites that are central to the songs of one *mada* as
contrasted with others. They also point to a larger territorial
range of common interests, in that some place names appear
in the songs of two or more *mada*. Clouds, for instance, are
not restricted to one stretch of country. They come from somewhere else and move on toward somewhere else. And so the
songs bring in place names, near and distant, outlining the
path of those particular clouds from the perspective of that
particular *mada*. Similarly for rain, bushfires, the shining paths
of the morning star and the moon, and other impersonal but
person-linked phenomena.

The overlapping series of place-names imply that some

mada have especially close links: 'Our tongues (*mada*) are separate, but we share songs'. In some examples the links are more explicit.

One is a *jiridja* 'fresh water' song cycle focusing on a major sacred symbol, a fallen log in a stream. In this case, it is a Dalwongu *mada* version. Toward the end of the cycle, after a crescendo of rain, little trickles of running water blend into small streams that fill and overflow and wash over sections of the country, and unite in one large stretch of water. Part of the *social* symbolism of this is the unity between various *jiridja* moiety *mada*. In one song, two streams from Dalwongu and Gobubingu territories combine: and people commenting on this added that there was a parallel in the social and ritual bonds between these two *mada*. In another song, the waters that merge into one come from Mararba, Ridarngu, and Wanguri as well as from Dalwongu country, and again the same parallel was drawn.

Jiridja moiety song-sequences like this one also contain references to *dua* moiety phenomena, and vice versa. They are deliberate references, underlining social and ritual links even more explicitly. For instance, in one of these songs the *jiridja* water washes around *dua* plants and trees; but in another it is the surface of the water that belongs to the *jiridja* moiety while the water underneath, moving at a different speed, is *dua*.

In other contexts a contrast is drawn between the alternating sequence of moiety affiliation through women and the in-variant sequence of moiety affiliation through men. A woman must always marry a man from the opposite moiety; and because the major emphasis is on patrilineal descent, any child she bears must be of his moiety, not hers. *Dua* women bear *jiridja* children, and vice versa. In songs focusing on the great shark of the *dua* moiety, the female shark carries a *jiridja* shark within her: and there are special words for this – for *jiridja-*

within-*dua*, and for *dua*-within-*jiridja*. Here, too, the practical implications of this symbolism are spelt out in the sphere of ritual collaboration.

The Dalwongu 'fresh water' song cycle illustrates another facet of social symbolism, symbolism with directly social relevance. The flood waters rush from one point to another, carrying before them all the small things they can dislodge – branches, leaves, grasses, little paperbark trees. But they do not (cannot?) dislodge the fallen log, which has been lying there from time immemorial. They swirl around it, cleaning and smoothing it without budging it in the slightest. The imagery is quite vivid. The log lies still and unmoving, while the songs detail the varied antics of the water all around it, the splashing and foaming and turmoil and the rushing of the streams laden with debris. Much of this is symbolically connected with specific features of human behaviour. For example, the foaming of the water is like the foaming of a man in a hot rage, preparing for a stylized but potentially deadly assault on someone against whom he has a grudge. But the broader, overall parallel is also quite explicit. It is the contrast between relative permanence or continuity, and change, both existing simultaneously and both necessary to life.

This contrast is expressed in a different verbal setting in the myth-linked sacred rituals that are concerned with human and natural fertility and with seasonal change – change within a framework of continuity. The principal myths associated with these are also shared between the moieties and more specific-ally between the various *mada*, and they exhibit the same pattern of territorial focus and spread. Occasionally they are told in narrative form, but most are sung.

Many minor characters appear in them, such as local spirit beings who 'always' live at certain places. In the *dua* bush fire song-sequences, for instance, the singer asks, 'Who lit that fire? Who set the grass alight so that flames sweep across the face of that country?' And he answers himself, singing their names, 'It is the spirit people of that country, always there, looking after it . . .'

But the most important characters stand out above all the others, in the sense that their names are known over wide areas and their actions are believed to have more far-reaching significance for human beings, and for living beings generally. Among them, to mention only the *dua* moiety, are the Djanggau (Djanggawul) Sisters, who came over the sea to the mainland coast in a bark canoe on the path of the rising sun and finally disappeared westward into the sunset; the Wawalag Sisters, who came north from the dry inland near the Roper River, and the great Python (a monsoon symbol, and also a phallic symbol) who swallowed them. The narratives and song-narratives that centre on these characters and on their *jiridja* moiety counterparts (who are actually less prominent) are made up of layers of interconnected symbols, in tremendous variety. The Djanggau Sisters created human beings and made waterholes (among other things), and carried an assortment of emblems, e.g. sacred feathered strings (which in some song-contexts are living birds, in others the rays of the sun), and conical plaited mats (womb-symbols) containing sacred ritual posts (phallic symbols). And their story accounts for the physical and social and ritual contrasts between men and women. In most of these sacred stories, either the actual song words vary according to the context or the words remain the same but the meanings vary. The most notable difference-in-context is between open, public singing in an ordinary camp situation and a closed, secret-sacred situation that is restricted to fully initiated men. In the last, the interpretation is more complex and the intermeshing of symbols far more intricate, with numerous cross-references to secret-sacred rituals.

The public singers in all ceremonial and ritual contexts are individual men from the particular *mada* concerned. They are expected to keep pretty closely to the traditionally conventional format and content, and their listeners are alert to any major variation – or, and this is much less likely to happen, any deviation. In practice, oblique differences in word-order and changes in minor words are quite normal. That applies also to women's singing – in their case, always individual and semi-private, and always on occasions of mourning or joy. They intersperse stretches of song with impromptu comments on the circumstances that occasioned it, making it very much a personal statement in addition to its social relevance. For men, room for personal expression is most obvious in the more everyday songs that deal with topical items of ordinary behaviour, composed and sung by individual men, but these are much less significant than in western Arnhem Land. Children's songs, or children's versions of the *mada* songs, allow scope for this too. And the 'play stories' told to children by adults, including junior versions of the sacred myths, can be dramatic performances in themselves.

The songs and myths and ordinary stories reveal a detailed practical knowledge of the natural environment and the skills appropriate to gaining a living from it. The north-eastern Arnhem Landers, like other Aboriginal Australians, are (and were traditionally) realistic and hard-headed on the score of economic potentialities. But they were also aware that this knowledge was not enough to meet all contingencies that might arise, through human action or through 'act of god' – floods, accidents, drought, death. So, over and above the translation of the songs into the social dimension, its parallels and symbolism, an essential part of them is the dimension of the non-empirical: the sphere of religion, of the sacred, including the secret-sacred.

5

In New Guinea

NEW GUINEA has had a more chequered history. And it has its own mixture of diversity and similarities (traditionally, as in Aboriginal Australia, *not* unity) – in terrain as well as in the life-styles of its peoples. Even in the temperate highlands, language differences mark off neighbours in adjacent valleys or on adjacent hill tops.

One point of resemblance to Aboriginal Australia is the emphasis on kinship, in relations between the members of a particular group, as one criterion in distinguishing them from outsiders (of various kinds) and as a fundamental guide to behaviour among themselves. Another is that in New Guinea too, men are dominant in sacred ritual, and especially in a zone of secret-sacred affairs which they keep strictly separate from women and uninitiated boys. Also, a few isolated peoples subsist on hunting and food gathering; but for most of them this is a supplement, if they engage in it at all. Sago is a staple in many low-lying swampy areas, and fishing almost a full-time occupation along the coasts. But, in contrast to Aboriginal Australia, the great majority are gardeners and pig tenders – gardens based on plot rotation, in what was at one time called a system of slash-and-burn or shifting cultivation (shifting within a fairly limited territorial range). And warfare, including head-hunting in some areas, cannibalism in others, was a central theme, that took up a great deal of their time, energy and resources.

Warfare and trade were the two principal avenues of communication between neighbouring groups, and both of these provided a major incentive for colourful display – in weapons, personal adornment, and ceremony. Also, some myths and stories as well as ceremonial elements can be traced in widely separated as well as in adjoining regions, and in very different settings – a promising field of study for diffusionists.

The area we want to focus on here is in the eastern Highlands, in what was formerly the trust territory of New Guinea, now administered by Australia under United Nations supervision. This particular region, south of Kainantu, was first visited by an Administration patrol in 1946, following the second World War. We were fortunate in being able to carry out anthropological research there in 1951–3, at a time when the northern villages and hamlets had been officially declared to be 'under control' but the southern areas had not. Warfare, sorcery accusations and cannibalism were still continuing in the south. In the north too – and this distinction is a rather arbitrary one, because we can't go into details here – government control was still too recent to have had much effect, beyond obvious effects like the cessation of open warfare, especially since it was mediated largely through native police from the Administration post at Kainantu.

Changes in the region since that time have been very rapid indeed. One reason, of course, has been the dramatic political and economic restructuring that has gone on in the Territory of Papua–New Guinea as a whole since the earlier, exploratory phases. Another, more specific, is the fact that the southern part of the area has been a focus of world-wide medical interest, because it is the 'home' of a unique disease syndrome for which there is, at present, no known cure. (Locally, it is identified as an especially deadly type of sorcery.) A research and treatment clinic has been established there, but so far the answer to it remains elusive.

At the time we were there, however, ordinary ceremonies were quite frequent. The important religious rituals centring on fertility, the cult of the sacred (secret-sacred) flutes, and the drawing of blood from various parts of the body, among other things, were continuing almost without interruption. Arrows, carefully shaped and decorated, were part of a man's routine equipment, with his heavy bow: and it was during our visit that the main shift took place from stone axes to steel.

Training for aggression was almost as important as fertility, in religious belief and action and its extension into the everyday world, with individual strength and well-being emphasized at least as much as group welfare. The rationale for this orientation toward physical aggressiveness and war was spelt out in two, mutually reinforcing modes. Warfare offered the ideal opportunity for men to display their strength and, symbolically, their virility: 'It is good that men should fight!' But it was also, they insisted, absolutely essential to their personal and social survival, and this belief was reiterated when Australian government patrol officers, coming into the region, urged them to lay down their arms and make peace with one another. In effect, '*We* would, but we know the others won't – and we have to protect ourselves.' The combination of these two kinds of justification meant that in very many instances offence was taken to be the best form of defence: and mythology supported this claim.

The principal creation myths here tell of an ancestral woman, often called Yugumishanta, and her husband, often called Morofonu, who made the first people and settled them in this area. They established the major language divisions, and they instituted sacred ritual. Mostly they are described as being in human shape, but they appear in other manifestations too: for example, Morofonu is a red parrot. The fertility theme in religion centred most conspicuously on garden crops and pigs, but obliquely on human beings (and other creatures), and on the life-giving, life-manifesting power of blood, especially of human beings or pigs, or both. Yugumishanta is the earth: and blood splashed on the earth is a libation to her, to ensure the continuing growth of all these things. The dead, or their bones, were traditionally buried in gardens for the same purpose.

Yugumishanta and her husband are also said to have been responsible for a large assortment of stories or, as we call them, secondary myths. The actual telling of these stories at the proper season continued the theme of fertility, as a rite designed to promote the growth of garden crops. And it was also explicitly described as a device for ensuring that local traditions were handed on from one generation to another. People likened the stories to two separate varieties of leafy plants. They said, of one, 'It holds the earth together on steep slopes and keeps it from crumbling – and so these stories hold us together'. Of the other, 'No matter what fires burn over it, it always comes up green and fresh, and so these stories will continue through each generation of people'. In contrast to the creation myths, these set out in story form the right and the wrong ways of behaving in virtually all of the circumstances that people in that area were likely to encounter in the course of experience.

The creation myths make positive statements, telling how and why things came about as they did. The secondary myths actually do that too, but always in a negative framework. At the end of each story, the characters in it kill a pig, splash the blood over a croton cutting, and then plant it, saying something like this: 'We in the story did that, but human beings are not to!' Sometimes they add a short maxim, pointing out what human beings *ought* to do. For instance, if the story is about trouble between two brothers, the maxim may be,

'Brothers are not to quarrel . . .' But putting the stories into such a framework means that the way is left open for the story tellers, and their listeners, to choose which aspects are to be treated as 'wrong'. And this is especially obvious when the story teller does not add a maxim. In other words, whereas the creation myths – like their counterparts in Aboriginal Australia – simply make assertions, which people are expected to accept without question, the secondary myths suggest the possibility of alternative answers. They imply that the issues they raise are not finally resolved.

Much of the content of these secondary myths deals with relations between living people. But a large number of others express concern about man's place in nature, his relations with other living and non-living things. One of the questions that preoccupies these people has a very 'modern' ring: 'Where do we draw the line between human and non-human beings? What is the boundary between man and other living creatures?' But their answers, or tentative answers, to that question are phrased in terms of myth and symbolism. To look at a few examples – some stories centre on shape-changing characters who may take a variety of forms according to circumstances.

A girl follows a man home from an all-night ceremony because she finds him attractive, but he responds coyly; to escape her he changes into a leaf, an insect, a pool of water – and so on, until she forces him to resume human shape. There are actually two types of shape-changing stories. In one, as in this last, the story character was human to start with, or predominantly human. In the other, non-human characters try to behave as if they were human, and in so doing they threaten or interfere with *real* human beings. A vegetable marrow or a tree kills all the children in a village while their parents are away in the gardens, or a snail licks a man's foot. When these things are killed, blood flows from them like water – showing that they were not true marrows or trees or snails but were aspiring to become human. In myths that take this turn, the moral injunction which ends each story usually states that such behaviour is wrong: non-human creatures are not to behave as if they were human, they must act in ways appropriate to their particular place in the natural order of things: trees are for firewood or (hollowed out) for ovens, vegetable marrows are food, and so on. These secondary myths are not accepted literally to the same degree as the creation accounts are. Nevertheless, they are explicitly regarded as true, given, and not open to human manipulation. There is recognition that different people tell a story in slightly different ways, but it is still 'the same' story.

Apart from these two types of myth, the one resting on the other, there is another field of expression that has a direct bearing on our discussion, i.e. songs. We shall leave aside the songs associated directly with myth and ritual, since, as in the Australian Aboriginal case, this would lead us into far too detailed a discussion of symbolic meanings.

Secular songs present some difficulties in presentation too, as far as translation goes, but it is easier to single out a few of the least complicated examples. They are composed by men, women and children on occasions they find personally interesting or exciting, or at times when they just happen to feel like singing rather than talking. The most popular of them are taken up by other people who are attracted by their tunes or by their treatment of various themes. A really catchy song may travel for miles, even outside its own language area; and composers from smaller language-units, who are mostly bilingual, deliberately compose in one of the larger adjacent languages to give their songs a wider currency. They are very much like 'pop' songs in the way their popularity waxes and wanes. For a few weeks, more or less, one song might be heard almost everywhere, from individual persons working in their gardens or walking along the paths. Then it is supplanted by another, and so on – although many 'new' songs, perhaps most, are actually built on the basis of 'old' ones. Other attributes of 'pop' songs are relevant too, despite differences in social context.

The best opportunity for airing the songs in public is a non-sacred ceremony when people from a number of different areas come together. The occasion may be a marriage, a crop-harvesting celebration, a mortuary distribution, a peace-making rite, and so on, but there is always a feast of some sort and usually singing or dancing as well. Among the groups moving across the dancing ground, one man or woman starts up a song, and the rest of that group and then the whole assembly join in, until that song dwindles away and another begins.

Songs provide a conventional medium for the expression of sentiments that contrast quite sharply with the eastern High-landers' delight in physical violence. They are heavily laden with verbal imagery, which draws on the natural environment either as a topic in itself or as a means of alluding symbolically to human beings. Especially, they are figurative ways of talking about people, for example, comparing some-one to a star or a flower or a length of yellow orchid fibre. A child complains that her elder brother, slow in returning home, is being delayed by the women of a neighbouring village, who are wrapping him up in words just as twine is wound around a bobbin. A girl, urging her parents to arrange her betrothal, compares herself to a ripe fruit that should not be allowed to fall on the ground and decay without being eaten. This is deliberate use of language to achieve a dramatic effect. In a few instances it seems to be done more or less mechanically, in much the same way as we ourselves often take figurative language as literal language once we have become used to it. But for the most part there seems to be a fairly clear awareness of what is involved.

Many of the songs convey, directly or indirectly, messages to other people in whom the composer or some subsequent singer is interested. They represent a way of talking to or about people in something less prosaic than the language of everyday life. Personal affairs and interpersonal relations are their principal concern.

The subject matter of other songs is the non-human world, often addressed in personal terms. A man out hunting coloured birds looks back toward his home but cannot see it: his vision is blurred by a mist-shrouded hill and by tears in his own eyes as he thinks of his relatives and of his home waters, and he sings sadly, 'Move aside, hill, so I can see my home village!' A bird sitting in a tree is warned that the singer is about to shoot it with his arrow. A woman jokingly tells a little insect not to fly around her all the time, she doesn't want it, she has a human husband. Fern leaves are addressed as young girls. In one song, a man's sugarcane crop appears to him in a dream warning him that it is ready for cutting. Often, croton leaves are addressed as if they were almost human, or had some human qualities – an assumption which takes on story form in the secondary myths. In most cases, this is straightforward personification of creatures that are already regarded as living in much the same general fashion as human beings are: i.e. as subject to birth (or emergence from the ground), growth, senescence and, finally, decay and death. Animals, birds, reptiles, insects and plants appear much more often in this type of situation than do artifacts or inanimate 'things'. Some of this is also a way of talking about people, but some of it is not.

In these songs, and in the bark emblems that are made for dancing with at ceremonial times, the use of symbols and figures of speech, including personification, is both conscious and deliberate. Composers, and other singers who took up their songs, were emphatic about this in discussion. They were ready to explain the allusions and, where they felt it to be necessary, they elaborated on the distinction between literal and figurative meanings. 'We say this, but we mean that.' Or, 'I just put that in [a reference to a flower, or some other colourful image] to make the song sound good . . .' The 'stem' of any song is its main substance; its 'leaves' are the extra singing-sounds that accompany it, rather like the English 'tra la la'.

Here are four examples of the very simplest songs – slight, impromptu affairs, with a nice sense of rhythm, that present no obscurities in translation. They are all in the Kafé (Kamano) language except for the first, which is in Yaté; and we give the actual words in footnotes to show something of the balance and assonance in their sung versions.

> O sun, you're going down,*
>   Going down, down, down,
> Going down into your house,
>   Going down, down, down!

This was ascribed to a Henegaru man, singing as he looked at the sunset.

> This girl here, hallo!†
>   Whither do you go, do you go?
> To Orungkanítei,
>   I go, I go!

The composer made this song 'for nothing', prompted by an exchange of greetings during a chance meeting with a young

---

*   Jege 'o fráanei,
        Frafrafráanei,
     Nókafi fráanei,
        Frafrafráanei!
†   Ama-mofarahéi!
        Inántega nevungkéi, nevungkéi?
     Orungkaníteiga
        Nevu'néi, nevu'néi!

girl on a mountain track. It was not a 'sweetheart' song. In fact, he later married her sister.

In the next song* a man is grieving for his 'sister', a young woman still in her teens. Her husband had brought her before a local native court (of the kind discussed in R. M. Berndt in *Excess and Restraint*) to be publicly tried and punished for running away with another man. She was made to lie down in the centre of the village and thrashed with a bamboo cane; and while this was happening, the singer wept for her.

> My eye, is it a sweet thing that I see you?†
>   My ear, is it a sweet thing that I hear?
> On rough ground by the stream,‡ Green Bird, do I see you?
>   My eye, is it a sweet thing that I see you –
> Green Bird girl!

In the next song,§ men had been cutting down trees at Guza'i until finally only one was left. The singer looked at it, its branches creaking in the wind, and thought of the thick bush that had been there before: and he felt sad. A tree, like a man, should not stand alone – and lonely: it should have companions, for help and support. But there was another, more practical explanation, for his feeling of sadness: the trees

---

*   Navú haga-zanei kagétesuwei,
          Nagésa haga-zanei ntahítesuwei!
       Kerorimpina neneimakei'na, kagétesuwei!
          Navú haga-zanei kagétesuwei—
       Mofara, Neneiko!

† Lit., '(with) my eye, sweet-thing you – maybe I see' (subjunctive), '(with) my ear, sweet-thing maybe I hear', etc.

‡ This is the literal meaning, but it is also the name of the girl's home ground; and *neneimake*, an unidentified dark green bird, is also the 'meaning' of the girl's name.

§   Uri-karahéi, eri-karahéi
          Nehuno –
       Guza'i zafa'o!

and undergrowth had provided a good ambush-screen between two districts in time of war.

> It sways creaking,
>   That way and this way –
> Oh tree at Guza'i!

Of course, no culture is all of a piece. It contains all sorts of internal inconsistencies and contradictions as well as complementarities. The Eastern Highlanders were no exception in this respect.

They were callous and unfeeling in the excitement of war, to people they regarded as hostile or to members of other districts living among them whom they suspected of treachery. But they sympathized tearfully with one another in misfortune and had a strong sense of self pity. Courageous and fearless of danger at some times, they were timid or reluctant to be involved, at others, for fear of being hurt. Their training for aggression and war stressed the need for solidarity, for a united front. But they guarded jealously the right to 'opt out' on specified occasions – apart from conventional neutrality between individual kin on opposing sides in times of war, not everyone took part in any skirmish; and a boy who did not want to go through the more severe items of his initiation could take his time in agreeing to it. People were attached to their own territory and wept, thinking about it, when they were separated from it. In times of danger, especially, they reiterated that home was the only place where a person was really safe and secure. Yet (apart from enforced departures as wartime refugees when their villages were routed) they made journeys of up to several miles in search of wild betel nut or to hunt or trade for coloured birds. And, in myths, people would set off into the distance simply from curiosity, attracted by a drift of smoke. Conservative and tradition-bound in many respects, they eagerly sought new kinds of vegetables and other plants, traded down to them through their neighbours in the north, and new flowers to brighten their villages. Women's hands were rough and calloused from gardening, but they kept their hair braided and greased with pig fat and were careful about their best bark-strip skirts; men took special trouble with their hair-styles, using wooden head-rests to avoid disturbing their braids at night, and even for everyday purposes many of them included adornments like coloured feathers and seeds or the beak or entire body of a red parrot. And they planted, in their gardens and hamlets and along the mountain paths, crotons and succulents and coloured flowers, simply for decoration.

In case-history material and other reports on the past, two complementary themes keep recurring. One is the demand for the members of any social unit to stand together. When men of the same district were in serious conflict, somebody was likely to intervene, urging them to settle their differences before an enemy could take advantage of them. The other is the view that every person has a right to see himself (or herself) as an individual, not as simply a member of a social group. It constitutes recognition of the need for a margin of choice, a margin of freedom – even though in practice, as in all human societies, this extends only so far. The sphere of song-making, and ordinary ceremonial activity generally, allows the greatest scope for individual self-expression. People can choose their own personal adornment. Men can choose which emblems they want to make and their specific meaning, and whether or not they will join in staging one of the impromptu dramatic performances that are a feature of these ceremonies. In one song, a man underlined this 'right to privacy' more deliberately than usual. He took part, one evening, in a song-making session in a men's club-house, a time of relaxation when men discussed their songs – the context, the symbolism, in short, what they 'meant'. But then he sang one about himself, using the conventional image of a red parrot that symbolizes a handsome, pleasingly adorned, neatly groomed person, especially a man. Freely translated (substituting the word 'sing' for the literal translation, 'make' or 'say', because singing is understood), it went like this:

> Oh, about myself I am singing,
>> As a red parrot, I am singing,
>> Here at Kugufarekei, I am singing.

He refused to answer any questions about it, beyond saying 'I made it about myself. You don't understand me . . .'*

But outside the flexible ceremonial range, the right to exercise individual initiative carries with it the obligation to accept the consequences. If a person is strong enough to ensure that the consequences are in his favour, he can, or could, get away with a great deal. A weaker person had less latitude. And in most everyday courses of action, it was safest to stay well within the range of conformity.

* See C. H. Berndt, 'Ascription of Meaning in a Ceremonial Context . . .', in J. D. Freeman and W. R. Geddes, eds., *Anthropology in the South Seas*, Avery Press, New Plymouth, 1959, p. 178.

6

Similarities and Diversities

THESE glimpses into the traditional scene in Aboriginal Australia and New Guinea, slight as they are, have brought up a number of points that are directly relevant to our broader discussion. A few things remain to be said; but for this purpose we can look at the two regions together, with due attention to the differences as well as the similarities between them.

It is true that the imagery in all of the songs we have been talking about, in both regions, is derived almost entirely from nature while the sentiments and themes focus on people. But that was how they saw their world. Where the songs deal with man-made things, other than sacred paraphernalia in the religious sphere, they do so almost incidentally.

The Australian Aborigines, in particular, set little store on housing and shelters. And although many of their ordinary secular artifacts had personal value to them, they could replace these without too much effort, either from the basic resources around them or through trade and exchange. Even where sacred objects were concerned, much of the pleasure as well as the spiritual power or force associated with them came through the actual process of making them. A large proportion of them was destroyed immediately after use, or allowed to decay in the specific waterholes or specific sites that were mythically linked with them. Rock engravings and paintings have survived over very long periods, but this is 'planned survival' only where designs have been renewed or touched up, mainly for ritual reasons. In many examples, later designs have been superimposed on earlier forms, all but obliterating them.

New Guinea shows a greater concentration on material equipment and durable art forms, especially in art-rich areas like the Sepik River and the Rai Coast, including the striking decorations and imposing forms of the men's club houses. Nonetheless, much that was aesthetically pleasing to the people themselves (and to outsiders) was intentionally demolished. A very good illustration is F. E. Williams' *Drama of Orokolo**. The 'drama' is a ceremonial complex of the Elema people on the Gulf of Papua, centring on the making and display of large mask-emblems, the *hevehe*, in a cycle traditionally extending from ten to fifteen years. Williams' description of the final burning of the ceremonial masks that had taken so long to prepare is one of the most poignant in the literature – if not in its words, at least in the picture that it evokes. The women, he says, could not bear to watch: they turned and fled from the scene. 'Thus', as he puts it (p. 376), 'the products of years of industry and art perished in a few moments.' Allowing for the conventions – after all, that is what the women were *expected* to do – something of the emotion and drama of the event come through quite vividly. They were heightened, perhaps, because over the whole thing hung the shadow of a 'last performance'. Times had changed, the coming of Europeans to New Guinea had ramifying consequences, and the *hevehe* cycle might never be repeated.

In the ordinary way, however, traditionally speaking, in Aboriginal Australia and in New Guinea, the assumption was that people would continue to make the kinds of things that they had made before. Objects were disposed of, ceremonially

* Oxford, Clarendon Press, 1940.

or otherwise. But this was done on the understanding that new ones very much like the old, if not identical with them, would be made in due course. It was not 'obsolescence'. There was continuity as well as change. And this applied also to the songs.

In regard to sacred songs and sacred myths, the emphasis was on non-change. Some allowance was made for individual innovation, provided this was phrased in the right way – for example, minor modifications could be introduced as a result of dream-revelation. But this was, on the whole, a conservative area of behaviour and belief. Outside that range, songs came and went – composed, as the ceremonial emblems were, on the basis of past models, but with new and personal touches. Songs of individual composition did not flourish everywhere in Aboriginal Australia. But even where they did not, light-hearted song-and-dance sequences for relaxation and entertainment were an intrinsic part of everyday living, traded over long distances and nearly always undergoing some variation in the process.

In both of the regions we have been talking about, then, the most explicit emphasis was on continuity with the past. In the absence of writing, this emphasis was one means of drawing attention to the past as such. Certainly, the past was referred to as providing a plan, or blueprint, for human behaviour in the present. But myths and other backward-looking accounts contained enough references to 'supernatural' happenings that could not be repeated, and to wrong behaviour that should not be repeated, to underline the view that the past was *different* from the present. The implication was that the future could be different, too, from the past as well as from the present, if people did not take steps to ensure that it was not: and the steps they had to take were seen as being of two sorts – predominantly religious and ritual, but relying on the accepted modes of social control by human agents.

It would be easy to point out negative qualities in both of

these situations. As far as health and disease hazards went, their populations were very vulnerable: high death rates, the toll of disease and accident, inadequate medical knowledge, the small margin of protection against natural disasters. And their lack of reading and writing skills, and simple technology, set limits to their development along other lines.

Nevertheless, to look at them in this negative light is to see a dull and distorted reflection. On one hand, it hinders recognition of their positive qualities – the ordering of social relationships, with their stress on reciprocal obligations; the allowance for individual personality and individual variation within the overall pattern of convention and constraint; and the un-elaborate but imaginative and pleasing contours of their graphic and verbal and musical arts. On the other hand, it blurs the great diversity of socio-cultural arrangements within these two regions.

In Aboriginal Australia, and even more so in New Guinea, while we can speak of common themes, we are confronted even more conspicuously with a tremendous kaleidoscope of differences. As soon as one tries to look beyond first-level generalities, beyond the level of Aboriginal-Australia-as-a-whole and of New-Guinea-as-a-whole, the complexity of the actual situation becomes apparent. Labels like 'primitive society', 'primitive culture', 'tribal society', even the more neutral term 'non-literate societies', have the same blurring effect.

Both Aboriginal Australia and New Guinea represent virtually classic cases of people with territorially-bound conceptions of humanity.

Among Australian Aborigines, members of neighbouring groups came together for ceremonial and ritual gatherings, and trade and gift exchanges linked individual persons across tribal boundaries. In myth, some characters travelled over vast areas. Plains Kangaroo, and also the Two (Goanna) Men, moved over hundreds of miles in the Western Desert, for instance, leaving behind them sacred sites and other visible and tangible evidence of their presence. In fact, from the perspective of people in any given locality, the majority of such characters came from somewhere else and perhaps departed eventually for somewhere else, to places that these people might not know even by name.

This in itself points to an extension of social relationships outside that locality, and implies, to some extent, an open-ended view of social relationships. But most such groups were quite narrowly ethnocentric. In many instances, a people's name for themselves could be translated as 'human being', and their disparaging statements about others outside a certain range reflect the same assumption. Even the north-eastern Arnhem Landers, exposed over several centuries to the visits of trading praus from what is now Indonesia, used to jibe at the non-circumcizing people farther to the west and their incredible marriage practices, and the unintelligible 'bird-speech' of people away to the south. One set of rules applied within a tribe – ideas of proper behaviour, checks and restraints, all that goes with 'being human' in this localized sense. Another applied outside it.

In New Guinea the picture was even more sharply etched, thrown into relief by the ideology and practices associated with warfare. On one hand, groups in adjoining valleys might speak different and mutually unintelligible languages. On the other hand, raiding and war and headhunting parties ranged over great distances in some regions. Again, ideas of behaviour appropriate for and in relation to human beings were strictly localized – and, the ethos of such New Guinea societies being what it was, this included ideas on *humane* treatment. In most cases, within a certain territorial range people recognized themselves as bound by kin or local or other close bonds, governed by rules of 'no killing', 'no stealing', and so on.

Within a further territorial range, some rules applied, including warring and inter-marrying relations (varying, according to area). Outside it, in most cases, stretched the limitless zone of 'no rules at all', whose inhabitants were regarded with an indifference that went far beyond feelings of active hostility or antagonism. They were so totally outside the range of humanity that they simply did not count, except (in some areas) as suitable victims for exceptionally adventurous head-hunting expeditions.

Interestingly, one marked contrast between Aboriginal Australia and New Guinea has emerged in the contemporary scene. In New Guinea, hundreds of manifestations of what have been variously called cargo cults, millenarian movements, messianic movements, and so on, have been reported from almost the first period of contact with Europeans up to the present day.

In Aboriginal Australia, however, though the impact of Europeans was far more devastating, virtually nothing of the sort seems to have taken place until quite recently, and then in a very diluted form. Even in the north of the continent, Aborigines seemed to be giving way before the pressures of alien penetration as their world crumbled around them. It is not that they lacked traditional myths which could have underpinned such movements if socio-political conditions had been right. The north-eastern Arnhem Landers, for instance, have a cluster of traditional stories that account for the discrepancy between their own range of material things and the things possessed by outsiders – in this instance, Indonesians. Long ago, they say, a mythical character in the shape of a Dog came to the coast from somewhere inland and saw Macassan praus at anchor in a bay. Their crews offered him matches, but he refused: 'I have my firesticks!' They offered him a prau, but he refused: 'I have a canoe!' He would accept nothing from them, because he was content with what he had.

Here is the nucleus of a Melanesian-type 'cargo' myth, but it did not, apparently, develop into one. In the 1940s, it was treated as a humorous story. 'If Dog hadn't refused them, we would have had matches too!' – but this was a topic for laughter, not for protest. The coconuts and canoes that came with the north-east wind were 'gifts' sent by ghosts from one of the islands of the dead (of the *jiridja* moiety) to their living descendants: but this, again, was not followed up in any 'cargo' movement in response to European contact.

In other parts of Aboriginal Australia, mythical themes of despair and tragedy reflect the hardships of, especially, arid-zone ('Desert') living: but these are accepted as natural and inevitable, like their counterparts of satisfaction and pleasure. This is so even in western Arnhem Land, where hundreds of stories 'explain' the striking rock formations in the central Arnhem Land escarpment. They were people, mythical characters who were 'swallowed', individually and in small groups, by the great Rainbow Snake in a fury of storm and flood – mostly for something they had done wrong (such as flouting a tabu), but in any case because this was their destiny. In a few instances, a mythical person with a grudge against others deliberately smashed a tabu stone, involving himself as well as them in the inevitable disaster. (The only reported cases of suicide in Aboriginal Australia, traditionally, are in *myths* such as these.) But all of the characters involved live on in spirit form at the sites where they were swallowed or their bones were vomited by the Rainbow, making the land itself 'alive' for its human inhabitants. And the Rainbow is also a symbol of fertility, linked with the annual monsoon rains that bring new growth as well as sometimes disastrous floods.

Without our going into possible reasons for this, however, it is plain that Australian Aborigines in general have moved from apparent capitulation to political involvement without intermediate 'movements' of the Melanesian sort.

The New Guinea people, in contrast, were possibly just as religious, but certainly more politically restless and individually self-assertive. And they were geared to a more hostile social environment. They fought back aggressively; and, when that approach failed, they turned to 'supernatural' validation to assert their own right to the goods and esteem and political recognition that they wanted.

In the process of pacifying and 'civilizing' these remoter areas of New Guinea, warfare was forcibly suppressed. To the Eastern Highlanders, this was itself one of the accepted fortunes of war. They were used to defeats, just as they were used to triumphs, and to other possible outcomes in the course of their almost cyclical war-making 'games'. The only real difference, in their eyes, was this: that Europeans came from right outside the ordinary zone of shifting enmities and alliances, and were so powerful and so rich in material goods that they must have either superhuman qualities or extra-ordinary magical skills, or both. The local people believed, then, that if only they themselves could acquire the same qualities or skills, they could reverse their defeat and regain their old independence. Their secondary myths suggested that this kind of thing was possible: mythical persons who knew how to go about it in the right way were able to derive material and other benefits from characters who were just as unpredictable as Europeans. 'Cargo cult' and related manifestations in this area, therefore, had two facets. People took ritual precautions to protect themselves from the dangerous alien force embodied in Europeans. They chewed special leaves, for instance, and sacrificed pigs. And, also in ritual terms, they made one attempt after another to obtain *things*, and especially weapons such as rifles.

Basic to all this was the value they set on warfare as such. It was never haphazard. Individual attacks and offensives never took place without some kind of justification and, conversely, were never accepted as 'justified' by the people they were directed against. Nonetheless, in a general sense warfare was more than an existential reality. It was regarded as being positively good.

The official view, in the course of bringing these areas under Administration control, was directly contrary. It contended that warfare was morally wrong; that human life, including 'enemy' life, was in effect sacrosanct and not to be taken lightly; and that civilized men settled their differences through negotiation and discussion, not through violence. These sentiments were variously expressed. They were communicated to the local people through government officers, usually via interpreters, and the end-result was not necessarily an exact reflection of formal official policy.

What it amounted to, however, was that the New Guinea people were being asked (ordered) to conform with an ideal, not an actuality. The implication was, and is, that inter-district and inter-village warfare were morally reprehensible in a way that 'non-tribal', large-scale, warfare is not: that there was a qualitative difference between the two. But as these people become better acquainted with what is happening in the wider world outside New Guinea, they can be excused for looking askance at this official condemnation of their traditional past. A cynic might say that in practical terms the distinction actually hinges on the nature of the weapons, on the elaborateness of the accusations and counter-assertions and, in short, on the scale of the enterprise. Translated into the wider world scene, perhaps, are some facets of the New Guinea traditional scene writ large.

In brief, then, we have been looking at some facets of life among two peoples who are usually classified as lying well outside the range of 'civilization'. Neither of them has made much of an impact on the great metropolitan cultures which conquered them through a mixture of military and political force and relatively peaceful infiltration – rather, vice versa: fringe items like tourist materials, some traditional artifacts, a few bits of vocabulary, and so on, *in toto* very slight in comparison with what has been a predominantly one-way flow.

Our discussion focused on one kind of symbolic and aesthetic expression, with a sketch of its socio-cultural context – on the language of symbolism and poetry, in just enough depth to indicate what it involves. Anything more subtle would have led us into a fairly solid analysis of socio-cultural and linguistic detail – consideration of wit and humour, for instance, or the more intricate symbolism of religion, or the field of the graphic arts, or real poetry – which we glanced at in the north-eastern Arnhem Land examples, but not in regard to New Guinea.

In a number of respects, the New Guineans are closer to Europeans than the Australian Aborigines are: in their emphasis on material aspects of living, on aggressiveness, on individual self-assertiveness. Not that these qualities are (or were) lacking in Aboriginal Australia, but in New Guinea they are far more pronounced. Looking at them in this light, looking at similarities and differences here, we might even suggest that in one sense the Aborigines were more toward the 'civilized' end of the continuum, New Guinea further away from it, and our kind of society further away still. *In one sense* – remembering all that has been said about technical developments, material equipment, intellectual discovery, and scientific method. But is technology enough? And, again, as regards scientific method, is the contrast so complete?

Mythical thinking is not confined to organized religion, to formal manifestations in myths (and rites). In Aboriginal Australia and in New Guinea, although people had a sound and detailed appreciation of practical economic affairs and the use of human and natural resources, this was not independent of emotional, affective *and* mythical elements. Nor is its counterpart in Western societies. What is happening is not so much a move away from mythical thinking, as far as the great majority of ordinary people and a very large slice of their everyday living are concerned. It is, rather, a continuation of *almost* the same mixture in different combinations, without equivalent checks and balances in the social dimension – or with different checks, and stress on more impersonal sanctions. But that is touching on another range of issues.

One point of interest here, still continuing the theme of poetic and symbolic language and following it, not into the realms of poetry or aesthetics generally, but into the sphere of commerce, of 'practical economics', is the increase in technical know-how for interacting with and managing other people. Australian Aborigines were quite skilled at this, but the New Guineans worked harder at it, and in Western societies it is a full-time preoccupation of many specialists in a variety of professional fields. It includes mythical as well as 'rational' thinking – and improved techniques for drawing upon and taking advantage of emotional, non-rational, 'mythical' thinking as part of the content of the expanding systems of 'mass' and inter-personal communications.

PART 3

CONTENT AND MEDIA

7

The Many Faces of Myth

MYTHS in Aboriginal Australia and New Guinea (see Chapters 4, 5 and 6) are myths in the classic anthropological sense – what Malinowski called 'charters', guides to action: myth in a positive sense, considered in relation to its context. Malinowski spoke of functional relevance, the *function* of myth in any particular society. The word 'function' is under a cloud, these days, in social science. It has been used in so many, often inconsistent, ways that anthropologists and sociologists have become wary of it. Without going into the controversies surrounding it, we refer to it here simply to point out that, in this positive sense, myth is linked with the rules and norms and actual behaviour of the society in which it is accepted: and this is an intrinsic part of its definition. People believe in it, take it for granted, act upon it (or contrary to it) or cite it as an ideal or a possible basis for action. It is the belief-and-action dimension that counts, for the people concerned and for the anthropologist looking for a label (myth? folktale? fairytale? some other term?) that will most adequately convey, in translation, the words those people themselves use in referring to it.

In popular usage, though, myth does not have this meaning. It still has the connotation of belief, but the overriding stress is on falsity: myth is false belief, to be exploded or refuted or dismissed.*

Bidney has been the main champion of this view in Anthropology. 'Myth' he says†, 'originates wherever thought and imagination are employed uncritically or deliberately used to promote social delusion'. Myth 'must be taken seriously as a cultural force ... precisely in order that it may be gradually superseded in the interests of the advancement of truth and the growth of human intelligence. Normative, critical and scientific thought provides the only self-correcting means of combating the diffusion of myth ...'

Two disparate streams have converged to produce this criterion.

One rests on the widespread tendency to accord other people's beliefs, especially religious beliefs, a lesser standing than one's own. This is most noticeable when social-political as well as religious identification is at stake, but it is highlighted in missionary and similar proselytizing endeavour. In some circumstances it is, again, a matter of definition, almost tautologically so: other people's beliefs may be 'true, in a way' – but not of the same order of truth. The standards of evaluation in this kind of approach are fundamentally the

---

* To single out just one example, a newspaper item in 1969 headed 'Another Greek Myth', went on to say: 'The belief that they are among the world's biggest coffee drinkers has been disproved ...'

† D. Bidney, 'Myth, Symbolism, and Truth', in T. Sebeok, ed., *Myth: A Symposium*, American Folklore Society, Philadelphia, 1955, pp. 13, 14: also his *Theoretical Anthropology*, Columbia University Press, New York, 1953.

same as in myth: they are within the same universe of discourse.

The second approach, ideally at least, is not. This is assessment on the basis of scientific method and procedure – not on the basis of scientifically acquired knowledge, because by its very nature that is itself open to reappraisal and possible obsolescence. Bidney prefers to speak of *normative* scientific standards, and he has been the prime mover in urging anthropologists to adopt the criterion of false belief in defining myth.

But both approaches based on this criterion are approaches from *outside*: they represent an outside view. To start from the charter aspect is to start with an inside view – or, rather, a combination of both, since the inside view (or views) is mediated through outsiders' statements about it. Neither perspective (charter, or truth–falsity) has an advantage over the other when it comes to the search for generalizations within a broader comparative framework. This search for generalizations is part of accepted social scientific procedure, whatever the starting point – just as it is, though expressed in a different idiom there, from the standpoint of the humanities. 'False belief' and 'charter' are not, of course, mutually exclusive criteria. Nevertheless, many anthropologists prefer to retain the emphasis on charter, or function, on the grounds that the truth–falsity grid can be applied to any kind of verbal statement, including not only myth but also folktales and so on. All of these, looked at objectively, may contain both truth *and* falsity.

These issues are still important, and still contentious, but they are cross-cut by others. Attempts to define myth by including all of them are so vague as to be almost meaningless. Actually, virtually every discussion of myth includes or comprises a definition of it, explicitly or otherwise. Some writers have settled on a single aspect, such as 'myth deals with supernatural beings, deities, etc.', or, 'myths are sacred stories', or 'stories, etc., associated with sacred ritual' (myth as the 'verbal counterpart of ritual'), or 'stories, etc., concerned with origins' or set in the distant past. Others put together a loose bundle and call it 'myth-etc.', as we ourselves sometimes do. Or they bypass the issue of definition by using 'folktale' as a more neutral term, particularly if they are concerned with content rather than with socio-cultural context. But this evades the crucial issue of belief.

A case in point, where myth is not singled out as a special category, focuses on the origins or the diffusion of motifs or plots or themes or tales, in the field of oral literature generally. This was a major interest of the Finnish School of folklorists, and one outcome has been the formidable Aarne–Thompson motif-index of folktales. Over and above the search for universal themes in myth, it has been amply demonstrated that certain motifs, motif-clusters and story-complexes do have a very wide distribution indeed – not merely themes, such as the Cinderella theme, but specific motifs, plots and so on, in very dissimilar socio-cultural settings.

Many regional studies of myths and folktales, especially in the past, concentrated on recording and classifying material, without necessarily paying attention to local variations. If they asked the question, 'What differences are there?' or 'Why?', they tended to answer it in geographical terms – and likewise in regard to the question, 'Why similarities?' Some such studies were oriented explicitly or deliberately on diffusionist lines. But attention to regional distribution, and the study of local (contextual, personal) linkages, are not mutually exclusive. Both approaches can be combined in a single study.

Another kind of approach to 'origins' is the contention that myth originated in ritual. Raglan's name is most prominent here. The controversial issue in Raglan's stand is not whether there is some association between myth and ritual, because in many instances that is undoubtedly so, but the claim that all genuine myths must have (or must have had) a ritual basis. It does not dispose of the question of variation in myths (or rites) between one socio-cultural situation and another, but traces everything back to a set of simple basic assumptions, such as the life-giving aspect of ritual.*

Malinowski's 'social function' approach was not concerned with origins at all, or not explicitly so. (We could also speak of political, poetic, aesthetic and other functions.) His 'myth' was a 'pragmatic charter', both a precedent and a guide to action. Above all, it was 'an indispensable ingredient of all culture', 'constantly regenerated'.† (Ernst Cassirer was at first strongly influenced by Malinowski, but the rise of Nazi power in Germany, with its 'Aryan myth', convinced him that myth was a dangerous force which could not be evaluated neutrally. The 'falsity' side of the argument became correspondingly important to him. Hence his references to the dark and 'demonic' power of myth.‡)

Malinowski's small study of myth deals specifically with his main fieldwork area, the Trobriand Islands, off the eastern coast of New Guinea, and he drew all his examples from it. But what really interested him was myth-in-general. The Trobiand contribution to the general discussion lay in the fact that myth was a living tradition there, not just a verbal survival. The area (Kiriwina) was compact enough to enable Malinowski to be alerted quite early to its dynamic quality and to see how it related to actual people and groups of people.

* He summarizes his position in 'Myth and Ritual', in T. Sebeok, ed., *Myth: a Symposium*. S. E. Hyman, in 'The Ritual View of Myth and the Mythic,' ibid., sketches the development of this approach, including Jane Harrison's work on Greek myth.

† *Myth in Primitive Psychology*, 1954 ed., Doubleday, New York, pp. 101, 108, 146.

‡ *The Myth of the State*, Yale University Press, New Haven, 1950 (3rd printing), e.g. p. 280.

This realization excited him – all the more so, perhaps, because he had been introduced to Anthropology (and the study of myth) through Sir James Frazer's classic work *The Golden Bough*: and, fascinating as that still is, the customs it enumerates are certainly not shown in their social context.

It was on this point that Malinowski himself had something to say, something that is still worth listening to in spite of the carelessness of its wrappings – careless, because it is obscured by a certain amount of polemic and inconsistency. The mixture is heavily peppered with two of his favourite words, 'primitive' and 'savage'. But that aside, he tried to give his own message more of an emotional impact by attacking views he thought were wrong. To cite one of these, he denied quite vehemently that myth could have an 'explanatory' aspect. This was his response to earlier emphases on myth as a predominantly intellectual construction, resting on 'intellectual' explanation, for example, Tylor's.* Tylor referred to a 'myth-making stage' of human development – but he also recognized (p. 396) change and re-interpretation as a feature of myth. Malinowski also opposed Max Müller's 'philological' approach. So did Andrew Lang,† but Lang's own views are equally unacceptable today. R. Dorson provides a résumé of this era in mythical controversy, in 'The Eclipse of Solar Mythology'.‡ Cassirer§ too saw myth as closely linked with language; but, for him, language could not develop until it was freed from the emotionally distorting influence of myth. Malinowski's own account, however, makes it plain that the Trobrianders did draw on myth to explain all sorts of things, from natural phenomena to social relations.

* *Anthropology*, Macmillan, 1881, pp. 387–400.
† *Custom and Myth*, Longmans, 1893.
‡ In T. Sebeok ed., op. cit.
§ See especially his *Language and Myth*, Harper, Dover Books, New York, 1946 (1st pub. in German), pp. 85ff.

Actually, much of what social and cultural anthropologists have published in the field of mythology is at least indirectly in the Malinowskian tradition – though Malinowski's influence is often unacknowledged or denied or his point of view ostensibly rejected.* Such studies might be called neo-Malinowskian. Usually they focus on a specific theme or themes, and draw on myths-etc. as an extra dimension of inquiry. Instead of examining a total corpus of myth-material, they take a selection of myths and discuss them within a particular framework: 'cargo cult' and similar movements, or land claims, or descent systems, or the socialization of children, or other aspects of social relations.

The truth–falsity dimension need not emerge as an issue in such studies as long as they are concerned mainly with content, even on a cross-cultural basis (looking at the distribution of motifs, themes, etc.). It can come up in translating the terms people use for narrative and song material – because some translators settle for 'myth' in cases where they themselves think they can identify both belief *and* falsity. As soon as one starts talking about symbols, however, and the interpretation of symbols, it becomes much more salient.

Broadly, a symbol can be identified within the broad category of signs by its conscious or artificial character. Allowing for individual differences, its meaning is a matter of more or less common agreement within a given social environment. But various types of symbol, or symbolism, can be distinguished. One question is how far symbolic meanings are shared: what is their social range; how 'private' or 'public' is the interpretation of a particular symbol, recognizing this as a matter of 'personal accent' rather than as something wholly personal, since the social context is always relevant, at least in the *shaping* of meanings. (This is so even in cases of extreme

* e.g. in Edmund Leach's *Political Studies in Highland Burma*, Bell, 1954.

dissociation where the individualizing of interpretation seems to have proceeded to its farthest limits.)

Truth–falsity assessments rest on more than a simple content-check of specific items. For both Bidney and Cassirer, labelling such items as 'false' was merely a way of pointing to a more profound, and disturbing, aspect of myth – its identification with non-rational or irrational thought.

One criterion they employed, in examining this identification, was that of literal versus symbolic truth: how far do the people concerned, the people for whom a given myth is valid, take this as being an exact statement of what actually happened; how far do they insist that every bit of it, or almost every bit, is literally true? They are not allowed to have it both ways, although they can have variations within each way. If they express literal belief in it, whether or not they attach symbolic meanings to it too, this is the answer that counts in the conventional true–false assessment. The western Arnhem Landers, in Aboriginal Australia, *do* (or traditionally did) believe that the Rainbow is an actual existent as well as a storm and monsoon symbol. For them, these are two coherent facets of one belief. But there is a very interesting point here that relates to a basic inconsistency in Bidney's approach. It is still within the true–false framework, but in the climate of a clash between religious 'truths' rather than of a confrontation between myth and 'normative scientific standards'. Although the advance of scientific knowledge was continually pushing back the frontiers of the unknown, Bidney suggested, they were not likely to eliminate it within the foreseeable future. That area, therefore, lay outside the bounds of assessment in terms of truth and falsity, and within it he located Christianity – but none of the deities or supernaturals of the non-literate world. In other words, this is itself an illustration of the belief and commitment that are inherent in anthropological definitions of myth.

To return, however, to the question of literal-versus-symbolic interpretation, a topical illustration is the Biblical story of the creation of the world and of humankind, of Adam and Eve, and the Garden of Eden. This continues to be a source of disagreement within the Christian church itself. 'Fundamentalists' ('Bible Christians') insist on a literal interpretation. Others see it as a complex of symbolic statements, although they have not reached consensus on what the symbols actually mean. They are closer to agreement on what the symbols *don't* mean – on recognition of interpretations that to them lie well outside the range of what is conventionally and generally accepted as 'Christian'.

Partly outside the purely religious sphere, but overlapping it, is poetry – a field of symbolic language almost by definition. Allegories and fables are symbolic statements, too; but in the parallel that is often drawn between myth and poetry the reference is to a profounder truth, that is somehow more real and more valid than literal truth. (Not everyone accepts this ranking. Whitehead, for instance, did not: he gave unequivocal priority* to 'blunt', literal truth.)

A special case of 'symbolic' interpretation is the sphere of psycho-analysis. Translation of symbols here can bypass or ignore or overrride the socio-cultural context. The rationale is that this is a particular kind of translation, one that depends on the specialized training and skill of the translator, i.e., fundamentally, on a psycho-analytic approach. The emphasis is on unconscious symbolism: a symbol need not be either conscious or shared.

Divergences and disagreements within this approach (e.g. between Freudians, neo-Freudians, and Jungians) concern such issues as how 'arbitrary' the interpretation of symbols should be – what variables should be taken into account, how far

* *Adventures of Ideas*, Penguin Books, 1948 (1st published 1933, Cambridge Univ. Press), p. 288.

culture is seen as a modifying factor or influence, and how far they can be regarded as universal or almost so. Erich Fromm's* modified approach distinguishes conceptually between universal and other symbols in his study of the 'forgotten language' of myths and dreams, a 'symbolic language' common to all human beings everywhere, regardless of cultural and other differences ('the one universal language the human race has ever developed, the same for all cultures and throughout history'†); but in practice, his interpretations of, for example, the Oedipus myth and the story of Red Riding Hood also appear to be quite arbitrary. Others, however, go far beyond him in that respect, making interpretation dependent entirely on intuition or on having the right 'feeling' for myth-material. An interesting attempt to explore a situation not usually treated in this way is Sierksma's *Tibet's Terrifying Deities*.‡ In his analysis he looks quite carefully at the socio-cultural dimension, and is quite cautious in his claims. Even so, his discussion and conclusions need to be considered in conjunction and in comparison with other studies and other statements about that situation. Myth itself involves an emotional stance, a particular kind of approach. But we do not expect *analysis* of myth to proceed along the same lines, even though something of the sort may enter into it at the level of 'hunches', or intuitive perception of possible meanings – as a preliminary or subsidiary part of the procedure.

Even at the level of straightforward ethnographic reporting, two interrelated questions that anthropologists learn to ask in any situation ('How does he/she know?' and 'So what?') are immediately relevant, if only because of such factors as selectivity, and the 'personal equation'. (Conversely, comments on and criticisms of such reporting are subject to the same hazards.) These become correspondingly more critical when

* *The Forgotten Language*, Gollancz, 1952.
† ibid., p. 16. ‡ Mouton, The Hague, 1966.

DESCRIPTION OF THE PLATES

Plates 1 to 5. Bark Paintings from Western Arnhem Land, North Australia (Berndt Collection, University of Western Australia)

Similar figures and scenes are among the thousands of rock paintings on this western side of the Arnhem Land escarpment – where, however, in 1970 'the world's biggest uranium find' was reported, an event with serious implications for the future of these colourful and important rock galleries.

Plate 1. Food for Mimi Spirits

One of several bark paintings relating to the stick-thin Mimi spirits who are believed to live among the high rocks and caves. This is a stylized representation of a plant that provides their favourite root-food. Artist: Old Wurungulngul.

Plate 2. A Hunting Scene

Illustration for a story. The two partly human characters hold spears, fitted to their spearthrowers ready to fling. At their backs hang long baskets (made by a twining technique) to hold personal possessions. Artist: Manggudja.

Plate 3. A Tortoise Site

This is a pictorial statement about a particular site and the main mythical character associated with it. At the beginning of the world, long-necked freshwater Tortoise was a woman who kept a sacred ritual object in a cave (oval in top right-hand corner) surrounded by stringybark trees. Today her spirit lives on there. Stringybark trees hang over the water where one of her physical tortoise-manifestations is swimming. Artist: 'Young' Wurungulngul.

Plate 4. Snakes on a Rock

A more compressed statement relating to another site. In the story, a group of Snake ancestors came to a large round rock at this site. They polished it and arranged themselves across the top before turning into snake form, 'putting their picture' there on the rock. Artist: 'Young' Wurungulngul.

Plate 5. Design for Sorcery

In western Arnhem Land belief, a person bent on punishment or revenge can achieve this quite easily by drawing a figure of his intended victim on a rock wall and singing an appropriate spell. In everyday life this seems to be more of a threat than an actuality, kept alive by myths and stories – like the one illustrated here. This is a stylized representation of an unfaithful wife in a story who was killed by that means. The bird's head indicates that a bird was involved in the spell. Stingray spines protrude from her limbs, symbolizing poison and pain, and her carrying-basket hangs at her back. Artist: Manggudja.

Plates 6 to 9. Bark Paintings from North-Eastern Arnhem Land, North Australia (Berndt Collection, University of Western Australia)

Plate 6. The Submerged Log

The sacred log mentioned in Chapter 4, in this case a Manggalili *mada* version at a specific site. The designs show freshwater springs and lily and grass roots (each side, and small right-centre panel), rocks, fish, a bird, and clouds with falling rain (the three central shapes): and a band of white dust (small left-centre panel). Artist: Naradjin.

Plate 7. A Coastal Scene

The designs include a salt-water tide-mark (horizontal band in right centre) with springs at each side, and running water marks, sea weed, lily roots and foliage, rat tracks and a dingo after rats, and white cranes searching for fish among the lilies. Artist: Nanjin.

Plate 8. An Indonesian ('Macassan') Prau

Indonesians were once familiar visitors to the Arnhem Land coast (see Chapter 4). This representation is on two planes: seen from above, looking down on to the deck, and also from the side, with sails unfurled, and attached canoes. Artist: Wonggu.

Plate 9. A Fishing Scene

Like most bark paintings of this sort, it should be looked at from several angles. The designs include reefs (vertical bands); two varieties of turtle, one eating starfish; seagulls and half-submerged tree; a canoe with four turtle-hunters and their paddles; and clouds (bottom left-hand corner). Artist: Mawulan.

Plates 10 (a) and (b). Secret-sacred Emblems in a Public Place: The Elcho Island 'Memorial', north-eastern Arnhem Land (see Chapter 6. Photos: R. M. Berndt). The 'Memorial' posts in their setting, at Elcho Island Mission station.

The posts and the designs they bear are associated with particular dialect group-clan combinations, and with specific myths. The large cross-topped emblem is, basically, the sacred submerged log (see Chapter 4): the cross is a symbol of Christianity, and the two together a deliberate attempt at syncretism. The attachments at each side represent bobbins such as women use for winding native twine. Other designs symbolize various fish, cycad palm leaves and nuts, and a special sacred stone. But in one sense the whole emblem is a mythical personage, the cross being his head and the bobbins his arms – one manifestation of the character in the centre foreground in 10(a), standing with arms raised above his head.

The large central pole in 10(a) is a whale-emblem; the designs symbolize parts of its body, and also fresh water, clouds (that take shape from its spray), anchor ropes and paddles, octopus, snakes, etc. The round-topped pole immediately below it on the right is an sun-emblem, the round top the sun's disc and the pointed spikes its rays, with designs relating to sunlight, phases of the sun, etc.

10(b) is a closer view of some of the emblems, showing the combination of realistic and stylized designs: e.g. in the foreground at right and second from left are tree-emblems bearing goanna designs, with conventional sandhill and plant symbols.

Over and above the aims that were made explicit in the 'Memorial' as such, the emblems and their designs show something of the intermeshing symbolism of north-eastern Arnhem Land songs and myths. They illustrate the surface of a more deeply layered system of meaning-within-meaning, the whole tied to a closely interconnected system of social units and social relations.

Plates 11 to 14. Ceremonial Scenes in the Eastern New Guinea Highlands (Photos, R. M. Berndt)

These photos were taken in the Usurufa-speaking district of Kogu in 1951-2, when Australian Administration control was quite recent and ceremonial life was still virtually unaffected (in marked contrast to the situation a few years later).

continued after plates

1 Food for Mimi
spirits

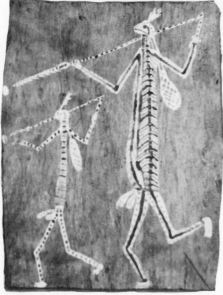

2 A hunting scene

3 A Tortoise site

4 Snakes on a rock

5 Design for sorcery

6 The submerged log

7 A Coastal scene

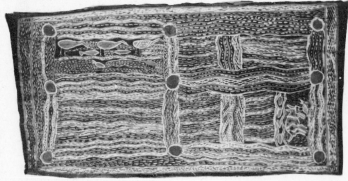

8 An Indonesian ('Macassan') prau

9 A fishing scene

10 Secret-sacred emblems in a public place: the Elcho Island 'Memorial', north-eastern Àrnhem Land

10(a)

10(b)

11 'Mother bird' and young

12 Dancers and emblems

13 Tableau and spectators

14 A pair of birds

15 Krishna and Radha on an elephant of milk-maids: Indian painting

16 Tradition and modernization: the temple of Yakushi-ji, Japan

Happiness is a folded paper in a chocolate box on top of the wardrobe.

17(a)

17 Happiness is . . .

happiness is a Monarch home

The comfort and security of a Monarch designed and built home can be yours for little deposit in any one of their modern new developments. Or Monarch will gladly build one of their modern designs on your own land for no deposit. They also have many delightful sites available for sale in their new spacious developments.

OPEN FOR INSPECTION TODAY, 1 to 5 p.m.

MONARCH

MONARCH CONSTRUCTIONS
196 Henley Beach Road, Torrensville, S.A. 5031
Phone 57 5139. After hours 43 1590, 65 1927, 66 2185.
Realty Division, Monarch Estates Pty Ltd. Licensed Land Agents.

17 (b)

PUT NEW **Life** IN YOUR LAWNS AND GARDENS

With **Top** BRAND

SPECIAL LAWN MANURES AND GARDEN FERTILIZERS

18 Flower children

Tiger, tiger . . .

19(b)

(a)

19(c)

Plate 11. 'Mother Bird' and Young

The headdress and mask of beaten bark are coloured white and pink with vegetable dyes, and the beak is a cowrie shell. The 'nest' with faces peeping from it is of leaves.

Plate 12. Dancers and Emblems

The dancers carry a mixture of traditional, formalized emblems and the more directly 'representative' variety that they have copied from other examples: innovation is a feature of such ceremonies. At the extreme left, for example, is the edge of a naturalistic bird emblem, a small animal on the right, and a 'handkerchief' in the centre; but in the right middle background the shield-like emblem on a dancer's back is a conventional *gopa'-agésa* emblem (a play on words: *gopa* is a water fowl, *agésa* is 'ear', but this bird itself has no ears . . .), and near it on the left a round daisy-patterned emblem also bears a conventional label – in this case, *kafi zafa*. Cassowary plumes are customary decorations, in ceremonial scenes and formerly in war-dress.

Plate 13. Tableau and Spectators

The three men in the centre with marks and decorations, one holding a drum, represent honey-sucking insects. The woman on the left carrying a switch is part of the tableau. (Round communal men's house and fowl coop in background.)

Plate 14. A Pair of Birds

Masked dancers with bird headdresses; the triangular designs at each side are 'leaves' of the trees in which they live. They beat drums as they dance. (Women's houses in the background.)

Plate 15. Krishna and Radha on an Elephant of Milkmaids: Indian Painting (Authors' collection)

Krishna, an incarnation of Vishnu, is the centre of many religious works (notably the Bhagavad-Gita) and the hero of innumerable episodes. In the second phase of his life, as a young man, he proved irresistible to the *gopis*, the milkmaids or cowgirls in the rural area of Mathura where he then lived; but Radha was his main love. The Krishna Lila, the 'love play' between Krishna and the *gopis*, has its more serious side, in the analogy of the human soul's devotion to God. But it includes also light-hearted, almost whimsical teasing and play – as in this episode, where the *gopis* form themselves into an elephant for Krishna and Radha to ride on. (A useful account of this part of the Krishna story is W. G. Archer's *The Loves of Krishna in Indian Painting and Poetry*, Allen & Unwin, 1957. Also, for example, M.S. Randhawa, *The Krishna Legend in Pahari Painting*, Lalit Kala Akadami, New Delhi, 1956.)

Plate 16. Tradition and Modernization: the East Pagoda of the Yakushi-ji Temple at Nara, Japan (Photo, R. M. Berndt).

This three-storied pagoda of the Hakuho art period (A.D. 645-710) is, according to Japanese tourist-literature, 'often described as "frozen music" because of its rythmically fine appearance'.

The blend of ancient and modern in today's Japan is reflected in the advertising of some of its export products. One example is an advertisement for the 'totally new Toyota Corona', 'The car that took 25 centuries to develop'. In its central illustration a Corona car stands in front of a temple pagoda, and the text underlines the combination of old and new techniques as well as of old and new aesthetics. (Other Toyota cars are promoted more prosaically: the Toyota Corolla 1100, for instance, as 'The Excitement Machine' – like the Mitsubishi Colt 1100, 'A little on the wild side'.)

Plates 17 to 20. Advertising for Adults

Plates 17(a) and (b). Happiness is . . .

Two variants on a popular theme. The first is about an insurance-company policy; the text modifies the 'chocolate box and wardrobe' suggestion and emphasizes the happiness-and-security of holding such a policy. The snail-house is also one in a series, a pumpkin-house being another. (Acknowledgements to the Australian Mutual Provident Insurance Company; and to Monarch Constructions.)

Plate 18. Flower Children

This combines a brand-symbol or 'trade mark' (a spinning top) and a pictorial image of plants enjoying their food, implying their dependence on human beings – in this case, a nurturing mother-figure. (Acknowledgements to Adelaide Chemical and Fertilizer Co.)

Plate 19(a), (b), (c). Tiger, tiger . . .

Tiger symbols are very versatile indeed. They are at home not only in poetry but in religion (e.g. in Mahayana Buddhism), in politics (riding a tiger, twisting a tiger's tail, a paper tiger) and in economics and commerce. 'A tiger for work' for example, can be merely a verbal statement, or this can be accompanied by drawing or an actual photograph of a tiger or tigerface.

The Esso tiger, with its constellation of verbal and pictorial imagery and its early slogans (e.g. 'Put a tiger in your tank!'), is an internationally famous character. The conventional 'horse-power' reference, that had been losing its figurative quality, has been revamped into a new and more powerful image. The combination of symbols is quite ingenious. It (or he) appears in a variety of styles, alone or in the company of human beings, in more or less straightforward tiger-shape. But as a 'tigerized car' he is a composite figure, a car that is a symbolic tiger. This imagery is a mixture of words and pictures: e.g. a small inset picture of a tamed-but-wild tigerized car behind bars carries such messages as 'Pad down to your dealer's cage today'. (For comparable examples see Chapter 9.) (Acknowledgements to Esso, and to Uniroyal S. A. Rubber. See B. Ash, *Tiger in Your Tank, The Anatomy of One Advertising Campaign*, Cassell, London, 1969.

Both 18 and 19, like 17(b), are in the direct tradition of children's book illustrations – using the simple imagery of straightforward personification.

Plate 20. Look After Your Car

The motor car as *almost* human (perhaps as an extension of its owner's ego, as some psychoanalysts would say), and also dependent on human care. (Acknowledgements to Caltex.)

Plate 21. War and Peace: a Perennial Dialogue

The theme is universal, and the time is always contemporary. Only the date-tag needs to be changed, forward or backward, to whichever year is 'now'. And the symbolic language conveys the message clearly, with a minimum of words. (By courtesy of Cedric Baxter, and of the *West Australian*, where it appeared on 28 December 1968.)

the language employed is persuasive and emotive – when there is an obvious jump between 'facts' and interpretation. However carefully and precisely a research design is formulated and the relevant data marshalled up with maximum attention to 'scientific' procedure, this kind of jump can still be involved. Other, and quite different ('non-scientific'), factors may intervene at the level of interpreting the data. The question, 'How does he know what the facts mean?' is especially pressing when conclusions appear to rest heavily on intuition and relate to unconscious, implicit, latent phenomena. This question has, therefore, been raised also in connection with Lévi-Strauss.*

In line with a widespread trend in other fields, such as componential analysis and transformational analysis (e.g. in regard to kinship and 'world view') and developments in structural linguistics, some studies of myth and folktales have been turning away from purely verbal analysis, description, presentation, and synthesis to specialized types of structural inquiry. These range from a search for patterns on the basis of word-counts or motif-arrangements, to more ambitious programmes such as the building of mathematical-type models with an eye on the computer.

Currently, the most famous name is that of Claude Lévi-Strauss. His 'new' look at myth has aroused the interest of philosophers and others as well as anthropologists. Although his own field of first-hand research is South America, and he turned back to that continent for his most detailed analyses, it is not his empirical findings that have gained for him so large a following, but his methodology. Starting with the fundamental premise that all myth rests on mediation between two irreconcilable oppositions, and taking as his unit of analysis, not individual elements but 'bundles of elements' (i.e. relations between elements), as in music, he has produced a brilliant array of structural patterns from a wide selection of

* E. Leach, *Lévi-Strauss*, Fontana, 1970.

socio-cultural settings. In addition, he has stimulated, or perhaps inspired would be a better word in some instances, a growing number of studies. Responses to these go all the way from complete and fervent acceptance to complete rejection, of procedure or interpretation or both. But the second point here (the first was the general question of 'how does he know?') is that, in trying to arrive at the underlying structure(s) of myth(s), Lévi-Strauss is concerned with showing the essential *intellectual* similarity of mankind, the so-called primitive along with the so-called civilized. As regards the content of myths, he pays special attention to social relations in the light of their socio-cultural context. As regards their construction, he turns to a wider, global, context to isolate common features that transcend socio-cultural divisions and demonstrate this basic intellectual commonalty.

Another facet of the truth–falsity issue is 'myth as history', myth as a 'true record of past events'. It includes the problem of archaeological substantiation of Biblical, especially Old Testament stories. This rests on precise procedures, these days, and dating techniques are becoming increasingly dependable. Nevertheless, a great deal still remains unaccounted for outside the range of purely material evidence, and there is room for the same jump in interpretation. Where archaeological investigations are not possible, or not relevant, material 'evidence' may be used in very much the same way as in Aboriginal Australia and New Guinea: i.e. sacred objects or features of landscape, like rock formations, as shown or cited as proof that the stories associated with them are true. When items in myth do not tally with observed, contemporary reality, some writers have tried to explain them as survivals from the past – the 'culture lag' idea. The notion of diffusion can come into this, for support or for opposition. But this kind of explanation has a lot of pitfalls, and usually a lot of guesswork.

And so we come to the issue of variation. The existence, and importance, of variation in myth (etc.) was recognized long before any systematic research was devoted to it. And the *Journal of American Folklore*, for instance, especially from the 1920s onward, includes a number of articles on it. One line of approach emphasizes the process of transmission, or the mechanisms involved in presenting one perspective rather than another. An alternative approach emphasizes the aspect of content. They are actually complementary, and to some extent overlapping, because they represent two facets of the multi-faceted question, '*Who* is saying *what*, to whom . . .?'

In cases where the telling or hearing of myth is divided up on the basis of age or sex or social status, as it is in Aboriginal Australia and New Guinea, we would expect differing versions to go with these divisions – or, at least, we would expect to find beliefs that there were such differences. This is over and above variation on the basis of personal choice within such a framework, or partly within it but also helping to modify it.

Of course, the personal dimension is always significant – personality factors, personal experience, a person-within-a-situation, interpreting, assessing, interacting with and influencing others. Each person is a point of potential change in a society – any society. A number of studies of variation in myth and similar material have concentrated on this dimension, or at least taken it into account.

Leach, in his *Political Systems of Highland Burma*, stressed the variability of myth as a statement of socio-political relations, where content was dependent on context, i.e. on the perspective of the persons and the social units concerned. He was not concerned with persons-as-individuals, but with persons in status, prestige and power relationships. In general, the tremendous assortment of myth-material, and of discussion that has accumulated around it, reveal this quite plainly.

Variation in form or content in different situations and in different societies, in the same society at different periods, or in different sections of the same society, is nothing out of the ordinary. It is an intrinsic feature of myth.

Let us look at a few examples.

In the great Hindu epic, the Ramayana, the central character is Rama, an incarnation of Vishnu; and the villain is Ravana, abductor of Rama's wife. Milton Singer cites a South Indian interpretation where the positions of Rama and Ravana are reversed in a deliberate attempt at 'de-Sanskritization', a reaction against the supposed dominance of the Sanskrit-influenced north: i.e. Rama is the villain, Ravana the hero. *The Illustrated Weekly of India* has had several perceptive articles on this theme of gods and goddesses in current politics and commerce. One, on 'Telugu Literature', asked who was the hero in Ranganatha's Ramayana, for Ravana was glorified in it to an 'unusual degree'. It has also been suggested that the positions of Rama and Ravana are reversed in parts of Ceylon – which, after all, is 'Lanka', Ravana's island home.

J. Radhakrishnan reported that in Java in 1945-9 'the stage-play Sandiwara' assumed 'a place of national importance in the popular imagination as the most effective media [*sic*] of mass propaganda', with 'classical characters' taking on 'new designations in the era of national struggle. Thus Ravana, the ten-headed demon, was depicted as the symbol of fascism, imperialism and colonialism. The ever-popular Pandavas [five brothers] of the Mahabharata became symbolic of the [five] Pantja Sila principles as Foundations of Free Indonesia'.*

Similarly, the Hindu god Ganapati (Ganesa) is shown as being concerned with live political issues in the contemporary

* This was in a feature article in *News and Views Indonesia*, Vol. II, No. 7, 1957, Embassy of Indonesia, Canberra, A.C.T.

scene.* 'The Chinese invasion provided the motif for the images of Ganapati this year, and Lord Ganapati was seen in many brave, patriotic and anti-Chinese postures. I am not altogether happy about the liberties people take when fashioning the images of Ganapati: and I feel particularly perturbed when I find Ganapati adopting the postures of popular film stars. But because people take such liberties, the images reveal the way in which their minds are working. What they revealed this time was healthy and reassuring, and Ganapati educated the people with far more imagination than is done by All India Radio.' And during the 1965 India–Pakistan conflict, several letters to the Indian press compared this with the great struggle between Rama and Ravana – with India as the modern Rama. (As one put it, the 'real Ravana' was Pakistan.)

Jacques Ellul† claims that, in our highly industrialized society, there has been a change in the kind of problem that myths are concerned with: that 'today the two fundamental myths of modern man are history and science', and that the focus of modern myths is on the origin of the machine, etc., rather than on the creation of the world. Since then, developments in space research, including moon-landings, have heralded a new era – or so we have been told: and, perhaps, a new mythological focus?

The Ganapati case shows a deity actively embroiled in current politics without losing his religious aura – if anything, the reverse. There were precedents in his particular role, including earlier involvement in the Indian independence movement. And he was (is) sustained by religious ritual on one hand, a 'company of believers' on the other – two factors that are responsible also for sustaining the Rama–Ravana

* Feature article, 'The Bombay Beat', signed Bahurupee. *Illustrated Weekly of India*, Vol. LXXXIV, No. 38, 22 September 1963, p. 19.
† 'Modern Myths', *Diogenes*, No. 23, Fall 1958.

contrast. Hundreds of other examples could be cited, from within as well as outside the Indian subcontinent.

But in probably at least as many instances the process has been one of secularization – for example, the persistence of Biblical stories and symbols in other than Biblical or religious contexts. Adam and Eve, Noah's Ark, and the Ten Commandments, like Red Riding Hood and Humpty Dumpty, are perennially renewed, perennially 'relevant', in messages – usually non-religious messages – presented through the mass media. And deities can be active in the commercial world too, as brand images in advertising. Ganapati, as one *Illustrated Weekly of India* writer observed, 'can be represented wearing a Gandhi cap or a waterproof wrist-watch'.

Myth, then, is *relative*. It has many faces. It changes through time, and at any one time it can exist in different versions and convey different messages. It says, in effect, '*Truth* is relative, it depends on where one stands'. (Cultural relativism and the sociology of knowledge again.) '*This* version is right, therefore *that* version can't be. . . .' From the viewpoint of the insider – the believer – myth embodies absolute truths: it is closed to further inquiry, as far as its basic core is concerned. From the viewpoint of a truth–falsity scrutineer, these two facets, individually or together, are in sharp contrast to the generalizing, universalizing, open-ended approach that is, ideally, characteristic of science.

But if myth varies within and between situations, so do outside perspectives on it. In the first case, the question is 'Who is telling the myth, and in what circumstances?' The answer, preferably, takes into account local observations on both of these points. In the second case, the question is 'Who is looking at the myth and the circumstances of telling, from some vantage point outside it? And, again, in what circumstances?'

If only because of its symbolic implications, myth-material lends itself to a variety of possible interpretations, and the questions or the categories of inquiry that an investigator brings to it can shape his conclusions in advance. Nevertheless, monistic explanations are still current, of myth in general and of particular examples, and this despite reminders that alternative possibilities are always worth considering. F. Bartlett suggested years ago* that 'a story chosen to illustrate one tendency, principle, or characteristic, will be found to illustrate half-a dozen others equally well'. Cassirer† did the same. The 'magic mirror of myth', he warned, reflects the interests of those who look into it rather than any intrinsic qualities of its own. The point is illustrated neatly by F. C. Crews in a 'take-off' of heavy-handed approaches to myth and story material, in a series of interpretations of the Winnie-the-Pooh stories.‡

Another issue that has to be taken into account in looking at myth is its relationship to its context – whether, and how, it reflects or influences the social order or culture context or individual behaviour and attitudes. This issue used to be treated, and to some extent it still is, as if the world of myth-etc. fell into two separate compartments that were the concern of different specialists: on one hand, the non-literate world, and material resting largely on oral ('word of mouth') transmission; on the other, written literature, mostly but not only of the 'Western' world, and the whole field of literary criticism – which we are not touching on here. This distinction is useful for certain purposes, but it was pursued so thoroughly that material which could with advantage have been considered together has been more or less arbitarily separated.

'Reflection' as such is fairly easy to document, up to a point. Available references are very numerous indeed. They range

* *Psychology in Primitive Culture*, Cambridge University Press, 1923, p. 59.
† *Myth of the State*, p. 6.
‡ *The Pooh Perplex. A Freshman Casebook*, Dutton Paperback, 1965.

from inclusive statements such as Hobhouse's* that 'the tales of a people reflect the general character of their ideas' to specific, itemized documents. But this is easier when the comparisons deal with tangible, visible materials. Assessment of 'values' and their reflection in myth is more complicated.

Systematic 'reflection' studies involve, ideally, both a complete content analysis of the myth-material in question *and* a complete ethnographic study of the socio-cultural situation. Like political cartoons, myths are not self-contained, complete in themselves. To be understood, they must be seen in context.

Connections between myth, religion, and moral values have been well established in principle, even though the nature of that connection varies – and notwithstanding controversies. Myth can be, and is, a repository of 'ought' statements – a source of moral rules, a guide to conduct, illustrating or pointing out the right way to behave in various circumstances, religious and otherwise (Malinowski's 'charter'). It plays an important part in the socialization of children. But myth can be, and is, a repository of 'ought not' statements, and this too is a part of the 'charter' aspect. Characters in myth often appear to go contrary to accepted rules, and to behave in ways that people in everyday life are discouraged or prohibited from imitating.

In Aboriginal Australia, for example, a myth may show over-familiarity between mother-in-law and son-in-law; incest; conflict, aggression and treachery in social relationships that ideally maximize solidarity and co-operation – and so on. In north-eastern Arnhem Land, the Djanggau (Djanggawul) and Kunapipi myths contain some striking instances of wrong behaviour. Warner, in *A Black Civilization*, gives a number of stories where this kind of thing happens, including one about a man and his mother-in-law. We recorded a very similar story,

* L. T. Hobhouse, *Morals in Evolution*, Chapman and Hall, 1951 (1st pub. 1906), p. 389.

but in that case the dominant theme was bad behaviour between two brothers and the mother-in-law element was incidental. This two-antagonistic-brothers theme is widespread, and not only in Aboriginal Australia and New Guinea. But in the north-eastern Arnhem Land example, explicit 'ought' statements associated with it lie outside the actual narrative, whereas in the eastern New Guinea Highlands, in secondary myths, statements such as 'This is wrong, people are not to do this', are included in the narrative itself – even though what is wrong is not always specifically singled out. Another 'bad example' (an 'ought-not' statement, or series of such statements) from Aboriginal Australia, this time from western Arnhem Land, is the Yirawadbad myth. A man kills his betrothed wife, and this is legitimate because she rejected him. But he also kills her mother – and that is wrong, because she was his true, consanguineally related, mother-in-law (his *ngalgurng*); he should have behaved toward her with respect and constraint, but also helpfully and protectively.

Attempts to account for the bad-example aspects of myth-etc. have been going on for a long time without really getting much further. The name of Euhemerus used to be associated with them, especially with explanations that can cut both ways. On the one hand, 'The bad example is projected into the myth because people can't behave like that in real life'. Compensatory projection, compensatory wish-fulfilment in fantasy, wishful solutions, and intermediate catharsis through vicarious participation are among the suggestions put forward here. On the other hand, the opposite explanation: 'The bad example in myth reflects what actually happens in real life'.

Linton* claims that such 'patterns for misconduct' are universal. Malinowski reported that in the Trobriands myth 'generate(s) its own replicas and is often used to excuse and explain certain otherwise inexcusable breaches of tribal

* *Study of Man*, p. 433.

law'.* Vico,† taking up this problem in the Homeric poems, suggested that people were afraid the gods might disapprove of their bad behaviour, and that to avert this they attributed similar behaviour to the gods. But Rieu's explanation‡ was that Homer saw the gods as being neither entirely good nor entirely bad, but mixed good-and-bad, like human beings – in contrast to the Christian demarcation between good and evil, as exemplified in God and Satan.

The difficulty is not so much the actions themselves – the fact that they are locally defined as wrong actions – but the question of who is performing them. It is quite appropriate for a bad character to behave badly, and this merely helps to define his identity (although the broader issue still remains). What perturbs some believers, or at least strikes them as something that needs explaining, is the discrepancy in a number of instances between the god-like or superhuman qualities of a particular character, and the apparently wrong actions attributed to him. (And his vulnerability.) Not all of them are satisfied with statements like 'He is showing us what *not* to do', or 'He didn't want to seem too remote from us, and therefore deliberately included a few flaws'.

One solution that has been tried is the downgrading of the character concerned, on the grounds that his identity has been misunderstood or misrepresented, but this is not likely to be accepted if he is religiously well-entrenched – not by fervent believers. N. Chandrasekhara Aiyer's translation of the Valmiki *Ramayana*§ met with some opposition in India itself

* *The Sexual Life of Savages*, Routledge, 1939, p. 454.

† A. Caponigri, *Time and Idea. The Theory of History in Giambattista Vico*, Routledge, 1953, pp. 192–3; T. Bergin and M. Fisch, trans., *The New Science of Giambattista Vico* (trans. from 3rd ed., 1744), Cornell University Press, Ithaca, 1948, pp. 270, 292. Vico also tried to reconstruct the far distant past of the Greeks from the Homeric poems.

‡ In his translation of *The Odyssey*, Penguin Books, 1954: p. 15.

§ Bharatiya Vidya Bhavan, Bombay, 1954.

because he asked 'whether Sri Rama was an avatar or incarnation of God, or . . . an ordinary mortal' (p. xiii), and found merit in the second of these interpretations since it 'enables us to get over and explain some of the alleged defects in the hero's life and conduct' (p. xv). C. Rajagopalachari, in his translation of the *Mahabharata** also refers to the principal characters in it as 'godlike heroes'. Of course, there can be other reasons for wanting to reinterpret the nature of a religious personage. Demythologizing need not mean secularizing, if the aim is to reaffirm the sacredness of the characters and events concerned by separating out basic truths from unnecessary accretions. Debates within Christianity on this score spread over into other issues that do involve secularization, e.g. the issue of historicity: whether Jesus was 'only a man', or Someone who was incarnated as a man for a divine purpose.

To Georges Gurvitch,† myth participates in shaping its socio-cultural context and at the same time is produced by that context. This is Malinowski exactly, though framed in a different idiom. But it is easier to speak generally of possible connections, or lack of them, than to demonstrate a clear-cut causal linkage in any particular case between myth-etc. on one hand and a specific course of action (etc.) on the other. The issue is simplest in regard to magico-religious rites, but far more complicated outside them. Even if people themselves report such a linkage – 'We do this because [such-and-such a myth] said we should' – this is only one kind of evidence, and it may actually be quite misleading.

None of the issues we have been talking about is confined to myth as against other narrative material, or to orally-transmitted as contrasted with written material. One of the few writers who has tried to bring together this usually-fragmented

* Bharatiya Vidya Bhavan, Bombay, 1950/1953.
† *Sociology of Law*, Kegan Paul, 1947, e.g. pp. 32-3, 37.

field is Milton Albrecht.* He identified (p. 525) 'reflection, influence, and social control' as the three main facets of the relationship between literature and its socio-cultural context, but under 'literature' he included myth. It is useful to have these facets summarized, but more so to have the beginnings of a conceptual framework that allows room for both the oral traditions of the non-literate world, and the written traditions and products and mass media of the Western world.

* 'The Relationship of Literature and Society', *American Journal of Sociology*, Vol. LIX, No. 5, 1954; also, 'Does Literature Reflect Common Values?' *American Sociological Review*, Vol. 21, No. 6, 1956.

8

The Personal and the Impersonal

THE term 'mass' has often been used in a pejorative sense, implying or specifying lack of differentiation – a dull, negative uniformity. Mass society is sometimes taken as synonymous with highly industrialized urbanized society, mass culture as its counterpart. Arguments on whether this 'mass culture' is a good thing or a bad thing reinforce the notion of uniformity, by treating it in those terms. But the trend now is toward identifying specific facets of it, and relating them to the social dimension – such as asking, Good or bad for *whom*? Two different views on the 'good or bad' controversy are outlined by B. Rosenberg and D. M. White, in the first two chapters of the volume they edited on *Mass Culture*.* Although this focuses on the United States (it is subtitled, 'The Popular Arts in America'), its coverage and treatment are wide enough to make it a good jumping-off point for further reading on all of the media that come under the 'mass' label.

Mass is a useful word, inasmuch as it draws attention to relative scale (of population and products), reproducibility, and so on, but it can give an entirely false impression. An audience or an assembly of spectators is never actually a 'mass' in a sense of being undifferentiated. MacIver and Page,†

* Free Press of Glencoe, New York, 1957.
† *Society*, Macmillan, 1950, pp. 433–4.

for example, see it as a diffused, dispersed, but at the same time 'ever-changing area of *specialized* . . . audiences' or 'publics'. Milton Singer, investigating 'The Great Tradition in a Metropolitan Centre: Madras',* commented on the 'maximizing' of audiences, in contrast to the smaller and more directly accessible and identifiable groups at the village level. He added (p. 357): '. . . the mass medium produces an impersonal record – on paper, wax, wire, tape or film – which exists separately from both performer and audience and can be mechanically reproduced. This makes it possible to send the program to mass audiences quickly and in practically any location'.

We would expect then, at one extreme, an almost complete absence of audience participation. But we also expect to be able to identify different (although overlapping) audiences or publics in respect of various media, within as well as between them: for instance, in cinema, radio and television, subdivisions on the basis of different types of film and B.B.C. (or A.B.C.) versus commercial channels, and so on. Within these publics, however, are other subdivisions, in this case providing scope for drawing people together on a more personal basis – linking them in communities of interest, including ephemeral groups or quasi-groups. One example is 'the jazz community' as sketched by A. Merriam and R. Mack,† made up of professionals and their public and marked off from outsiders by distinctive characteristics, including a specialized vocabulary. Fan clubs are another – clusters of localized groupings, each centred on some celebrity such as a film star or a singer. These provide the nucleus of the gatherings that assemble to meet (or see or hear or touch) their particular celebrity in person, and these gatherings in turn help to recruit more club mem-

* In *Traditional India: Structure and Change*, American Folklore Society, 1958.

† In *Social Forces*, Vol. 38, No. 3, 1960.

bers. Some have a quasi-religious, sect-like quality, reaching a peak of emotional fervour when devotees come together in the presence of their current idol. Radio and television stations, particularly those dependent on commercial sponsors, often take a special interest in sponsoring or instigating such gatherings (record sales supply one incentive for this). But this is only one aspect of their effort to establish the appearance of a directly personal relationship between announcers and listeners or viewers – using personal names and items of personal experience as deliberate steps in this process, encouraging telephone calls and correspondence, arranging entertainments where 'You will meet . . .' such-and-such an announcer in a friendly, convivial setting.

Listeners and viewers, especially the lonely and the elderly or the bored, are more than ready to respond – or *some* of them are. Jokes about people ('old ladies', usually) who are embarrassed about undressing in front of a television screen when the announcer is 'looking at them' point to this attitude of half-belief, sustained by programme statements such as 'Have us as a visitor in your home tonight!' (Cartoons showing interaction between film and television characters and viewers reinforce it too. For example, an election-time cartoon where a viewer, throwing an egg at the candidate on the T.V. screen, is disconcerted when the candidate throws one back at him – and his wife, sitting beside him, says, 'Surely you didn't expect him to just take it, dear?' Or a cinema scene, where a ragged character crawls from a dry, desert film-setting into the cinema itself, mouth open and tongue hanging out, toward a girl with a tray marked 'Drinks', while members of the audience sit watching him.) Horton* and others

* E.g. D. Horton and R. Wohl, 'Mass Communication and Para-social Interaction', *Psychiatry*, Vol. XIX, 1956, pp. 215–24; D. Horton and A. Strauss, 'Interaction in Audience-Participation Shows', *American Journal of Sociology*, Vol. LXII, No. 6, 1957.

have some interesting things to say on this topic of 'parasocial interaction'.

The issue of 'who-what-to-whom', i.e. of 'communicator-communication-audience' or vice versa, was summarized by B. Berelson in *Content Analysis in Communication Research.** These three categories are crucial, whether the content analysis is being done by human beings alone, or in conjunction with a computer – a trend that is currently popular and promises to be more so. It is absurd to imply, by the way, as R. A. Bauer does,† that 'who-what-to-whom' and similar expressions assume only a one-way line of influence and initiative. The framework of 'who-whom', etc., is basic to social inquiry, and none of its elements represents a fixed vantage point any more than it presupposes a fixed content.

Berelson also commented on 'reflection', and on variability in written material that claims to be a true record of the past but actually provides different versions of it according to 'who is talking', whose point of view is being presented, i.e. history-as-myth. Accounts of wars and battles in newspapers and also in history textbooks are among the most obvious examples. Nations formerly under colonial rule have a special interest in the re-writing or at least the re-framing of their history, affirming or re-affirming their particular national identity. The reinterpretation and 'correcting' of Indian history by Indians is a case in point, with the different light it sheds on such legendary episodes as the Indian Mutiny and the Black Hole of Calcutta. And, of course, the deletions and additions in public accounts of national events to suppress or re-slant the contributions of specific figures (e.g. Stalin and Khrushchev).

---

* Free Press, Glencoe, 1952, e.g. pp. 13, 26–7.

† 'Social Communication and the Influence Process', in S. H. Britt, ed., *Consumer Behavior and the Behavioral Sciences*, Wiley, New York, 1966. He was commenting on Lasswell's earlier formulation of 'Who says what. . .', etc.

For our purpose here, the 'who' question has two main facets. One is *control* or ownership of newspapers, magazines, radio and television networks, 'advertising time', and so on. Most of us probably do not need W. Albig* to tell us that there is 'a vast amount of conscious organization and manipulation of symbols in Western culture today', but his claim (p. 80) that allegiance to such 'transient symbols' is weak, that the 'very plethora of modern symbols diffuses attention', is more debatable. The second facet is *authorship*, the source of messages or media content. The actual or assumed source is highly significant, from 'outside' as well as 'inside' points of view. But a number of writers† have noted the widespread belief that a message is likely to be more effective if it is delivered by an expert or celebrity or prestige figure, whether or not he was originally responsible for it. This kind of sponsorship is especially popular in commercial advertising.

In the 1950s, some writers claimed to have discovered or rediscovered the importance of interpersonal communication networks. What they seem to have meant, was that the subject had been neglected in that particular field. To begin with, there had been an uncritical assumption that on one hand were the various mass media and on the other hand individual members of the public, and that the process of transmission and acceptance involved only these two kinds of agent. The possibility of intermediate, person-to-person transmission within this process was largely overlooked. But increasing attention is being paid now to patterns (e.g. 'chains', 'wheels', and concentric or centrifugal circles) of *personal* contacts.

E. Katz and P. Lazarsfeld‡ summarize attempts to integrate mass media research with small group research (p. 8). They

---

* *Modern Public Opinion*, McGraw-Hill, 1956, p. 79.

† E.g. C. Hovland *et al.*, *Communication and Persuasion*, Yale University Press, New Haven, 1953, p. 19.

‡ *Personal Influence*, Free Press, Glencoe, 1955.

discuss the rediscovery of the primary group (pp. 33–4), interpersonal relationships, primary groups 'as channels for mass media transmission' (i.e. their 'relay function') and also as serving to 'either counteract or reinforce their message' (i.e. their 'reinforcement function'), and the 'sharing of opinions and attitudes' (pp. 44–5).

Katz took up the same problem in relation to research in rural sociology and in the field of mass media. He concluded that, 'In both urban and rural settings personal influence appears to be more effective in gaining acceptance for change than are the mass media or other types of influence' (p. 439), and that these media should be viewed, not 'as competitive but, rather, as complementary [to personal influences] by virtue of their function in various phases of an individual's decision'.* D. C. Miller† also saw two complementary facets here: 'Radio speeds the spread of a news item by its swift transmission to mass listeners, which activates rapid word-of-mouth communication lines'. In the same vein, Johnstone and Katz reported that 'musical tastes and preferences for particular songs and for particular disk jockeys are . . . anchored in relatively small groups of friends, suggesting that personal relations play an important role in musical fads and fashions'.‡ On the importance of informal leaders in transmission of news, rumours, etc., and in influencing response to ideas or goods,

* 'Communication Research and the Image of Society', *American Journal of Sociology*, Vol. LXV, No. 5, 1960, p. 440).

† 'A Research Note on Mass Communication', *American Sociological Review*, Vol. 10, No. 5, 1951, p. 244.

‡ 'Youth and Popular Music', *American Journal of Sociology*, Vol. LXII, No. 6, 1957, p. 563. See also D. Riesman, *Individualism Reconsidered . . .*, Free Press, 1954, Ch. 11; and Riesman, Glazer and Denney, *The Lonely Crowd*, Doubleday Anchor Book 1955, Ch. VII, Section II; D. Horton, 'The Dialogue of Courtship in Popular Songs', *American Journal of Sociology*, Vol. LXII, No. 6, 1957, p. 569, sees popular songs as a conventional conversational language for use in dating and courtship.

M. De Fleur and O. Larsen* urge the need to study the inter-personal networks concerned in the communication process, such as how far various 'kinds of persons select or change content as it is passed along, and . . . direct it to persons occupying different roles in the social structure'.

M. Janowitz† refers to involvement in local or community affairs even in an urban setting. And, an interesting point, R. Waterman claimed that obscene stories 'have a tendency to remain in the purely oral tradition' within a literate urban society, and that in such a society this kind of material is almost the last stronghold of purely oral transmission – if only because some of it is 'unprintable' and would be subject to censorship in any other medium.‡ But, in fact, there are other such strongholds in which oral transmission is dominant. Rumour and gossip are two of them, like 'grapevine' net-works. Another has been well documented, for Great Britain, in *The Lore and Language of Schoolchildren.*§ Children's games and songs that they learn from one another and not from adults show a striking stability and continuity coupled with an equally striking flair for innovation – a blend that it is not always possible to detail, as it was in the Opie study, with the help of written material.

All this is part of the same concern that is reflected in other areas of social scientific inquiry – a concern with informal social relations as well as with those that are more tightly structured, the delineation of smaller social environments that mediate between the individual person and the wider social system in which he is located.

* *The Flow of Information*, Harper, 1965, e.g. p. 265.

† *The Community Press in an Urban Setting*, Free Press, Glencoe, 1952, e.g. pp. 22, 23.

‡ 'The Role of Obscenity in the Folk Tales of the "Intellectual" Stratum of our Society', *Journal of American Folklore*, Vol. 62, No. 244, 1949.

§ I. and P. Opie, Oxford University Press, Oxford Paperback ed., 1967.

In urban studies, one form this inquiry takes is the exploring of kin and neighbourhood relations, the 'discovery' that kinship can still be important even in densely built-up areas, and consideration of the circumstances in which it is not. The place of the family in highly industrialized societies is another pertinent line of inquiry. So is the whole field of community studies, not least the endeavours of welfare and town planners to recapture or restore community in the ideal sense – community defined, not so much in terms of space but, above all, in terms of co-operative attitudes and behaviour, 'we-feeling', MacIver's 'community sentiment'. The heightened emphasis on *social* psychology, *social* psychiatry, *social* medicine, and so on, over the past few decades, is an indication of the same trend – a return, in a way, to the traditional anthropological interest in the socio-cultural context of persons, things, and ideas as a necessary corollary of any study.

Both interpersonal networks and lines of influence, then, as well as the larger and more impersonal or mechanical organization of messages, are relevant to the question of the influence or effects of various mass media – including the issue of censorship. One continuing argument focuses on the relationship between, especially, television programmes and delinquency. Sex and violence are major issues here, although there are others too. The central query is whether television programmes (or films or books, or magazines, or newspapers and so on) do more than *reflect* what is happening in the 'real' situation – do they instigate or precipitate or reinforce similar behaviour on the part of viewers, readers and listeners? Answers range from 'direct and positive effect' to 'no effect'. But there is also the question of *how* such influences operate: what is the connection, if any, between such material and the courses of action that people follow after seeing or listening to it? Among the factors that have been proposed are reinforcement of existing potentialities already latent in certain persons, or a predisposition to behave in certain ways rather than others. And, especially, the social environment in which people are exposed to such material.

What is particularly intriguing here is the disjunction between ideas about television (and other media) outside the setting of formal education, and ideas about television (etc.) within that setting. In the first, there are deep-seated disagreements on cause and effect connections, and some of the disputants have taken pains to justify their 'no influence' or 'minimal influence' stand. In the second, it is not that doubt is absent – hence the constant search for more effective teaching and learning procedures. But, overall, both practising and academic educationists seem to have a fair amount of confidence in what they are doing, and this presumably includes a conviction that, to spell it out, there is some positive cause and effect association between teaching and learning, and subsequent behaviour. The overlap, and the interstices, between these two fields – television (etc.) as entertainment, and television (etc.) as education – should be a source of illuminating generalizations, providing variables that can be isolated and controlled.

In Western European-type society, as far as censorship goes, the section of the population regarded as being 'at risk' seems to be its children and adolescents.

On this, P. M. Pickard makes three points in *I could a Tale Unfold. Violence, Horror and Sensationalism in Stories for Children* – especially small children.* One is that 'horror' material is firmly established, and accepted, in classic adult literature – a point that is well known but sometimes forgotten. The second is that children need to have such material explicitly discussed with them and brought into the open because their own fantasies include it. More needs to be said about this, taking into account material from other cultural

* Tavistock Press, 1961.

settings. That aside, it has a parallel in the notion of 'children as savages'. The third point is also familiar and also needs underlining, i.e. that a person's response to an event can vary, according to how he interprets the emotional climate in which he experiences it – for example, as reassuring or threatening. Children, then, can take a great deal, provided the setting of a story and the way it is told help them to cope with this mixture of aggressiveness, guilt and fear instead of suppressing it: 'Nothing is really too bad for them to hear about, since the terrible basic plots are already within them; what matters is how they hear about such things' (p. 190).

The question of what is there already, by way of fantasies and fears of aggression, and how these fantasies can be 'worked out' to ensure adequate personality development (which is what this involves), overlaps with another and more general question – the presentation of *any* such material, children's stories or adult fiction and drama.

Dramatic structure necessitates some sort of plot, some sort of conflict, if a story-line is to hold the attention of listeners or readers. As the heading of a press review of the Pickard book put it, 'What Good are Goodies without Baddies?' The good example makes sense only if it is contrasted with the bad example. And, as Durkheim has said, this is always a relative matter, if only because of the inevitable gap between ideal and actual performance. (In *The Rules of Sociological Method*, his example of 'sin in a monastery' was designed to show that, even in an environment emphasizing piety, or perhaps because of that emphasis, one would always expect to find offences and, especially, definition of offences.) One reason that some of the most sacred Australian Aboriginal myths are hard to 'put across' to outsiders is that they do not depend on this dramatic structuring or that they approach it differently. Their main concentration is on relations with the land and on particular ritual complexes, and, although they contain plenty of small dramas, the plot aspect is very much subordinated. They are not stories in the way that many of the less sacred myths are, and so their appeal is more specialized as far as non-Aborigines are concerned.

Even the more slow-moving myths, however, include the dramatic highlighting of clash and conflict and wrong behaviour. And whenever this happens, whenever we find the use of the 'bad', whatever that is, to point up the 'good', there is always the problem of how both of these will be interpreted and translated into action. The dramatic form itself helps to perpetuate the bad example as a guide to potential behaviour; and the onus for defining it (as good or bad) and handling it at the level of overt action, is thrown back on to the social environment, the socio-cultural context.

In the New Guinea situation we looked at in Chapter 5, it is not only the secondary myths that illustrate in graphic detail what *not* to do. Traditionally, information on this score was always included in the initiation rites that were designed to turn boys into socially effective adults. By the time they were eight or nine years old, they had already left their mothers' huts to join their fathers in the men's houses that were a part of every village or hamlet-cluster – because men and women always slept and ate separately. In local ideology, supported and validated through myth, men were courageous, aggressive warriors, not afraid of anything that other men might do to them: but, although other men could be dangerous, women were very much more so. A woman could weaken a man, destroying his strength without even meaning to do so, and this threat was much harder to combat than open violence. In individual instances and in general statements about ideal behaviour, affection between mother and son, brother and sister, first cousins, husband and wife, and so on, is amply documented. But the theme of basic mistrust between males and females pervades almost the entire range of actual and possible relations between them, and the assumption is, or was, up to the time we were living in that area, that men cannot learn about this too early.

When a group of little boys is assembled in a men's house during their initiation programme, this is one of the things they are taught: 'Be careful in your relations with women and girls.' Men would stage short dramatic scenes, illustrating the main kinds of wrong behaviour. In one scene, a man commits adultery with his elder brother's wife – and is shot for doing so. In another, a man steals from a garden in his own village, and is soundly beaten. In another, a man is ill, on the point of dying: 'He has been weakened through too much association with women' – an association that is weakening in itself, especially if it involves accepting food from a woman in a tabu-state, but can also make him vulnerable to sorcery (black magic). In all such scenes, the boys are told, 'This is wrong. You are not to do this.' But they are also told, in effect, '*If* you do this you will suffer, you will lose your strength, you may die – but it's up to you. Take the risk if you want to, but you see what will happen to you!'

On the other hand, in the large festive gatherings when people meet for singing and dancing and emblem-displays, much the same scenes are put on for entertainment, along with compressed dramatic episodes from the secondary myths. These include much ad-libbing and topical comment on the part of the actors – but never any reminder that the behaviour they are illustrating is formally regarded as wrong. The liveliest scenes typically concentrate on the bad example, and of these the most popular are on sexual themes. And at all of them, the most avid and untiring of the spectators are children, especially boys. Little boys push to the front of the crowd to watch a mock-adultery scene, in which a man assaults his 'wife' (always a male actor) whom he has caught *in flagrante* with her lover, or a scene in which two 'women' importune their weak husband who is tearfully unable to cope with them, or another in which an elderly 'woman' is seduced against her will. They laugh appreciatively at every repetition of episodes like these, with their symbolic gestures (flicking the bark strands of a 'woman's' skirt or crawling between her legs is enough to suggest sexual intercourse), and even more uproariously at the rather blatant phallic representations that are the *pièces de résistance* in some scenes.

In other words, in the formal setting of initiation the 'bad example' is explicitly treated as such, as something to be taken seriously and likely to entail certain sanctions. In the public setting of the ceremonial assemblies it is treated as comic and dashing – as 'good-bad' behaviour, not really reprehensible and not necessarily to be avoided. These two have a parallel in a third type of setting, this time in the public punishment scenes associated with the informal courts – as in the 'Green Bird girl' song mentioned in Chapter 5. Such courts flourished during the period when the region had been officially declared to be under government control but that control had not yet been consolidated. Armed warfare had been suppressed but men's feeling for it had not. Something of this interest in physical aggression, as well as their attitude of still being masters of their own destiny, found expression in these trial-and-punishment sequences, that were quite separate from the formal courts controlled by the Australian administration. Again, sexual offences were especially popular, though not the only matters they dealt with. But here the performances were live and the actions were real – no symbolic gestures, but a straightforward representation of whatever it was that the men in charge of the informal court had ordered. As punishment for adultery, for instance, the guilty couple might be forced to repeat their offence in public: 'You did it secretly before, now let us watch you!' Or the young woman concerned (rarely, older woman) might be stripped of her bark skirts and paraded naked through a number of villages, while her custodians called people from their gardens to come and look. In quite a few of these examples, the 'victim' took on something of the air of a celebrity – especially in the adultery cases, where the applause that greeted a successful performance was even more appreciative than for its symbolic counterpart on the ceremonial ground. And here too, little boys were among the most ardent spectators.

Aboriginal Australia, to turn to the second region we looked at (in Chapter 4), has nothing quite like this. Ordinary ceremonial scenes, even those dealing with sweetheart-affairs, are much more decorous. Sexual relations, closely simulated or real, are never acted out as a public spectacle to provide entertainment, though there are plenty of symbolic allusions to them in appropriate song-series. In everyday life, they are expected to take place in private. In the context of magico-religious or secret-sacred ritual there are symbolic and occasionally actual performances, but these are never embarked on lightly and the ritual context itself stipulates and defines the seriousness of their intent.

Nevertheless, in Australia as in New Guinea, children become acquainted very early indeed with almost all aspects of relations between men and women, in broad outline, and this includes fairly detailed information on physical, specifically sexual matters. Many of the stories that they hear, and are told, are quite explicit about these. And their own observations, the things they see and hear and ask about, fill in the gaps. Although adults, ideally, behave with propriety – it would be in very bad taste for a husband and wife to touch each other even fleetingly in public, for instance – there is no suggestion that children should be sheltered from the facts of adult living. The situation is one of learning and teaching, preparing children for roles that they are not yet ready to take up. The only scenes that are forbidden to them, as far as this is concerned, are in the context of ritual and religiously based tabus: men's secret-sacred affairs, and the huts or shelters where women are periodically secluded, including the circumstances of childbirth. In Aboriginal Australia, although physical violence does enter into occasions like camp fights, it is minimal in comparison with New Guinea. Nor are there the same opportunities for personal observation and personal involvement in this kind of activity. But, in both, children traditionally witnessed and participated in the total round of everyday life, not excluding illness, accident and death – and, in the New Guinea case, the bloody shootings and physical devastation and refugee-movements of local warfare. In fact, such real-life examples were deliberately kept fresh in a boy's memory by constant reiteration, to ensure that he would be ready to play his part when he was old enough to fight: 'They killed your father!' – or brother, or sister, or first cousin. 'They drove us from our land and destroyed our homes!' And so on. And, since the rules of good behaviour applied almost entirely within a fairly localized range, restless young men who had been trained for war could always be deflected from going on a rampage in their own village area, by setting off to burn a house or steal a pig in another place that happened to be an enemy at the time – or provoking it to become an enemy.

Children's exposure to sex and violence in dramatized or fictional form – and in real life – is not something associated only with Western European society. Nor is it new there – not by any means. In most places, at most periods, it has been anything but unusual. But it has always taken place within a framework of understanding about rules and norms of behaviour, a framework of social control.

Questions of right and wrong, good and bad example, have always been linked with social boundaries, determining the limits within which sanctions could be imposed – rewards for good behaviour, punishment or threat of punishment for bad. And, a related question, what proportion of 'sex and violence' is regarded as tolerable or sufficient – how much, in relation to other things: and what other things? And what is the value orientation implicit, or explicit, in its presentation? Is there any formal or other requirement that the good example must be shown as superior or more desirable, as a more attractive course to follow? (e.g. amplifying the slogan, 'Crime does not pay'). And this brings us back to the question of 'who'. Who is responsible for establishing and co-ordinating these rules? Or, if responsibility is pushed further back in time or on to some supernatural authority – and myth and legal procedure have a great deal in common, in their recourse to established precedent – who is delegated to police them, or to adjudicate, or to make decisions on 'trouble cases' as the occasion demands?

The matter of adult censorship will come up again presently, but for the moment let us continue to look (in Chapter 9) at this topic of children – what is considered appropriate for them, what should they be sheltered from, what would be harmful for them, particularly in the sphere of the mass media.

PART 4

THE NEW BARBARIANS

9

New Wine in Old Bottles

(OR the other way round, depending on which aspect we regard as content and which as container, or vehicle.)

Sex and violence are, of course, not the only topics to receive the active attention of censors. Politics is at least as important, even if it does not attract the same degree of publicity, but it is only obliquely relevant to children. So is the politically sensitive field of race relations, pushed into the limelight by 'trouble cases' (such as 'Alf Garnett's' attitudes in 'Till Death Us Do Part'), that bear on the unresolved issue of how much in the way of real-life comments can or should be transmitted through the mass media.

A fifth topic was the subject of an interesting controversy in Australia in 1957. This centred on fairies and other 'make-believe' characters. The Australian Broadcasting Commission, in its 'Kindergarten of the Air' sessions, refused to accept or to broadcast stories about 'fairies, gnomes and goblins' in programmes for pre-school children, on the grounds that they were not sufficiently mature to understand them as older children could. One spokesman, according to Press reports, added that 'kindergarten listeners preferred animals, machinery and concrete mixers that talk'. Another claimed that they 'had not enough grasp of reality to understand fantasy' – in effect, that they were not yet able to understand or to use symbolic language. It was in this climate of opinion that Enid Blyton's 'Noddy' books were banned by a number of children's libraries in Australia. And the same theme continues to recur, for example in a 1964 press report from a spokesman for a London publishing firm dealing in children's books, to the effect that 'fantasy and fairy stories are definitely "old hat" as far as British children are concerned'.

It may be true, as some writers have suggested, that many of the classic fairy stories (like nursery rhymes) are not really children's fare at all – that it takes an adult to appreciate them and that is why, unlike children's lore (as in the Opie study), they are always, or almost always, handed on from adults to children and not between children themselves. But whatever the merits of that argument, fairytales and folktales now also serve adult audiences, or rather, adult readers, in a rather different context. In this they are a mode of communication between adults, on the assumption that adults will know enough of their content to understand what is being said and to interpret their message. Quite often, the message takes the form of a comment on political issues of the day, and the *dramatis personae* are the human protagonists in various current events, thinly disguised as traditional story characters.

In 1961, for instance, an Illingworth *Daily Mail* cartoon drew on the Red Riding Hood theme, slightly modified. The wolf-as-granny, Khrushchev-faced, in a bed bearing a hammer and sickle emblem, is smoking a pipe that emits a large 'mushroom cloud'; six Little Red Riding Hoods, recoiling from the sight, bear the faces of Sukarno and Makarios, for instance, with Nehru clutching at Nasser who carries the basket; and the caption reads 'THE AWAKENING – "And what a great big pipe you're smoking, Gran'ma . . ."'. Red Riding Hood appears again in a 1960 London *Evening Standard* cartoon, one of three over the inclusive caption 'Vicky's Panto Season', but this time the message has to do with Britain's entry into the European Common Market: Red Riding Hood, carrying a basket marked 'Exports', asks a wolf with an Adenauer face, 'I say, old boy, can you show me the way out of the wood?' And the sub-caption reads, ' "In-the-Red" Riding Hood (A Grim Tale).' The second of the three cartoons in the 'Panto Season' bundle (the third is 'The Sleepless Beauty', pillow bearing the initials, 'H.G.', 'looking for fellow-travellers under the bed') is 'Jack and the Beanstalk', with a giant labelled 'U.S. $-Crisis', and three Kennedy brothers climbing the beanstalk to a sign reading, 'Opening at the White House on January 20th'. In another European-Common-Market Red Riding Hood illustration (in a Punch cartoon repeated in the Australian press early in 1965), the disguised wolf in bed is de Gaulle and a timid, basket-carrying Red Riding Hood (with a Wilson face?) hesitates in the doorway: the caption reads, ' "Grandma" de Gaulle: "Come a little nearer, dearie".'

The Red Riding Hood theme has been used in popular songs, too. In one that has now vanished from the 'hit parade' charts, the singer (the woodcutter in the story?) begins 'Hey there, little Red Riding Hood!' and suggests that she really shouldn't go through those spooky old woods alone; he offers to accompany her to grandma's place. Wolf howls (animal) and wolf whistles (human) underline the dual meaning of 'wolf' in this setting. A story-version with a different twist, told ('by Stan Fribourg') at about the same time, is Little Blue Riding Hood. A 'cop' from the Narcotics Squad insists on seeing what a child in a blue riding hood is carrying in her basket. He finds only shotguns, rifles, etc. – nothing of consequence, and so she skips away. Then he discovers some hidden 'goodies', hurries to granny's house, sends her off to a psychiatrist and waits in disguise. The child arrives: 'Grandma, what a big subpoena you have in your pocket!' 'You and your grandma are operating a goodies ring!...'

The story themes, then, like the Noah's Ark and other Biblical themes that frequently serve the same purpose, are more or less constant – altered to some extent, but retaining enough substance to make it clear which story is involved. Their messages are more transient and so are the characters who convey them; the gallery of faces becomes, in time, like a 'who's who' without a key and mostly without names. The mixture is a blend of renewal and obsolescence. In the Indian myth-example we noted in Chapter 7, Ganapati keeps his identity while political events like the Chinese invasion wash around him: but *his* image receives constant support in the religious sphere. For fairytales and folktales, that does not apply, and in fact the number of stories that can be used in this way – in cartoon-comments – does not seem to be very large.

It is not only the political figures and events in the cartoons that are time- and locality-bound. The traditional story-themes that serve as pegs for them are also limited in their socio-cultural range. They are taught and learned within that range. Outside it, allowing for the distribution and convergence we mentioned before, they are meaningless or almost so. (Albig, in *Modern Public Opinion*, p. 399, looking at cartoon pictures over a 35-year period, reported that these were 'decreasingly self-explanatory'.) In another type of cartoon that is non-political in content, not geared to current events, the fairy story or folktale itself is the focus – and, again, understanding the message depends on knowing something about its plot and its main characters; but the general intention is similar – to give a fresh twist to an old story.

For one example, we turn back to Red Riding Hood, in this case combined with the widespread mother-in-law joke. In a Paton cartoon of the 1950s, a man is reading to a child in bed, from a book labelled 'Red Riding Hood'; their smiling faces contrast with the scowl of an older woman, the surprised displeasure of a younger one, looking at him through the doorway, as he reads: 'Then the nice wolf ate up nasty old Grandma and had stomach ache ever after.' The second example, in three versions, is the 'Frog Prince'. In one (unsigned: it appeared in the Australian press in 1963), two men are walking along a path toward a high, turreted fairytale castle, beside a 'For Sale' sign; one man, with a bundle of papers under his arm, says to the other (bow tie, interested expression, obviously a prospective client): 'Reason for selling? The owner was turned into a frog.' In another (also unsigned: 1968 in the Australian press), four characters sit on benches in a stone, lead-light-windowed room under a sign 'Ye Marriage Guidance office', around a rough wooden table holding a copy of *Punch*; two of them, a woman with ringlets and a mob cap and a man with bobbed hair and a short-sleeved tunic, are staring at the other two – a girl with long fair hair, a long, elegant dress and a crown, a tear on her averted face and beside her a fat spotted frog wearing a larger crown. In the third Frog Prince example (a Middy cartoon; the Australian *Bulletin*, 29 March 1961), two frogs are sitting on the ground together, one listening while the other gestures emphatically with outstretched hand: 'We were practically married, had set the date. Then, so help me, he turned into a prince!'

If the frog prince was 'really human' and merely the victim of an enchantment, the frog girl he deserted in returning to human shape (in the last example) seems to have had no such pretensions. She comes under the same broad heading as the wolf in the traditional Red Riding Hood story and a host of other talking animals.

But there are differences among these animal-figures. The wolf traditionally keeps his basic wolf-characteristics: he is a carnivore living in his natural habitat in the deep forest, who talks to Red Riding Hood and adopts the granny-disguise only as a new kind of hunting technique. The wolf in the Three Little Pigs story also retains his wolf-quality. But the frog girl, also in her natural habitat, is shown as having human-type sentiments and observing a human-type custom (betrothal, setting of wedding date). In the same way, some cartoon dogs live almost as ordinary domestic pets in human households – almost, not quite. Fred Bassett is a shrewd observer of the habits of the human beings he lives with, but they do not realize this: his thoughts and his comments are not for them but only for the cartoon-readers (and for other dogs). Snoopy, on the other hand, in the Peanuts cartoon strip, not only has a rich fantasy life (as in his World War ace, anti-Red-Baron phase a few years ago, commemorated on record as 'Snoopy's Christmas') but he also communicates fairly effectively with the children around him – perhaps illustrating the view that children and dogs communicate more easily with one another than adults do with either.

Other animals, however, are set in a more-or-less-human material environment which they themselves control and manipulate. The Three Little Pigs live in houses; they also try to construct them, though only one succeeds. Another group of Little Pigs, in the nursery rhyme, go to market – or one of them does. The Three Bears share a house, sleep in beds, and eat porridge from bowls – so that Goldilocks expected to find people there, not bears. Other animals behave even more obviously like people while remaining in animal form – sometimes keeping their distinctive qualities (e.g. a fox has certain attributes that a rabbit does not – as in the Tar Baby, B'rer Fox, etc., stories), and sometimes moralizing along Aesop's Fables lines. If we see this as a movement from more natural to more artificial, then a further step in that direction is the Mickey Mouse, Donald Duck type of character. Mickey Mouse, especially, does not look quite like a mouse but more like the animated cartoon-strip character he is. Another step brings us to the talking machine, or the machine-that-has-feelings-too: to *non*-traditional characters like the Little Red Engine, Tommy Tractor, and Charlie the Concrete Mixer.

Most of these characters, including the last three, are conventionally expected to appeal directly to children – with the proviso already noted, regarding latent or superimposed meanings. The question of what content is most appropriate to what ages, in helping children to learn (generally and in relation to specific subjects), intermeshes with the question of how children themselves spontaneously categorize the various items in their natural and socio-cultural environment – the people, creatures and inanimate things there. Piaget's name is most often associated with this.

A major difficulty is that adult teaching of children begins virtually from the time of their birth. Much of what used to be called 'baby talk', for instance, is now recognized as being adult talk directed at children on the assumption that this was the only language they could understand. Of course, there is a basis of common sense here, when children's linguistic as well as conceptual abilities are so obviously restricted. This is acknowledged in other societies, too. In Aboriginal Australia as we mentioned in Chapter 4, song structure is deliberately simplified by adults for children. They do this in the field of language as well: for example, in north-eastern Arnhem Land, substituting 'g' for initial 'ng' on the grounds that small children find the 'ng' difficult in that position. But they are quite clear about what they are doing. They recognize that children have speech and grammatical problems and often speak unintelligibly – unintelligibly except where their mothers are concerned: and they consciously impose particular word forms in an effort to help overcome these. This is not baby-talk in the 'moo-cow', 'puff-puff' sense.

Over and above linguistic considerations, however, is the matter of concepts. Without going into Piaget's views, because that would involve discussion of the formidable body of comment, criticism and amplification that has built up around them, let us glance at a naïve formulation of a little more than twenty-five years ago. The author* was (given such a modest project, somewhat over-ambitiously) 'interested in the question of whether there is a unified law of religious development, valid for each and every human being', and in the process of this inquiry was (p. 115) 'able to discover' among young children a 'specific characteristic – the presence of fairytales. We therefore designated the stage of religious expression of the preschool age (three to six), in accordance with this specific characteristic, as the "Stage of the Fairy-Tale Form of Religion".' The conclusions reached were these: 'In a concrete approach to the educational problem presented by a child's religious development at the preschool age, it appears necessary to carry out the religious education of this earliest period in a fairy-tale style' (p. 120). And (p. 121), 'If we are to win for our youth real religious freedom – the right and the chance to choose for themselves – we must help them to perceive the voice of their innate religion. We realize that this would mean some change in the religious structure of the American civilization.'

The more recent argument *against* fairy-tales for preschool children, it will be recalled, was that children at that age were not sophisticated enough to deal with this particular kind of fantasy – that talking animals and talking machines, being visible and tangible, were more 'real', and therefore more appropriate aids in introducing children to the 'real world'.

* E. Harms, 'The Development of Religious Experience in Children', *American Journal of Sociology*, Vol. L, No. 2, 1944, pp. 112–22.

A third part of the argument seems to represent a minority view, at least in practice. This is the claim that children should be discouraged from employing any fantasies at all: that they should be taught from the very beginning to adopt a rational, scientific approach to life, and that adults who take a contrary stand are hindering their development. There is no way of testing these conflicting views through experiment and the use of control groups – not simply for ethical reasons, but also because too many variables are involved, including the variable of time (how long would one need for this – the span from birth to adolescence, or longer?).

Some writers have claimed that, as Ruth Benedict* once put it, 'In animistic belief and practice, . . . man created the universe in his own image. He extended his human attitudes toward his fellows to an anthropomorphic universe.' Others, without denying this, hold that 'since the scientific revolution, nature has been depersonalized'.† Lewis Mumford,‡ after suggesting that animism stands in the way of technical development, goes on (pp. 371–2) to discuss Sombart's claim 'that the clue to modern technology was the displacement of the organic and the living by the artificial and the mechanical'. 'Within technology itself', Mumford suggests, 'this process, in many departments, is being reversed: we are returning to the organic: at all events, we no longer regard the mechanical as all-embracing and all-sufficient'; and 'the organic image [may even take] the place of the mechanical one'.

A 'personalized' and personified approach to the world has long been a feature of adult teaching and children's learning, especially in practical situations of warning about danger to children from animals – or danger to animals from children:

* In F. Boas, ed., *General Anthropology*, Heath, Boston, 1938, p. 642.
† E.g. P. Gutkind, in W. L. Thomas, ed., *Man's Role in Changing the Face of the Earth*, Chicago University Press, 1956, p. 18.
‡ *Technics and Civilization*, Routledge, 1947 (1st pub. 1934), p. 33.

'kindness to animals', 'dogs and cats have feelings', and so on, admonitions often extended to plants and even to inanimate things. Talking about levels of maturity, as Piaget did, taking personification of inanimate things as a sign of immaturity and a non-adult level, does have a certain utility: but it begs a number of questions. (Personification and animism are also regarded as a sign of senescence – a retrogression from an adult level to a stage of senility.)

As against this, a glance in any reasonably stocked bookshop or library of books and other material for young children is likely to reveal a sizeable proportion of titles on exactly this sort of topic, i.e. not only animals (etc.) behaving like people, but also the personalizing of ships, engines and trains, and machines of various shapes, sizes and functions. And these books, with rare exceptions, are prepared for children by adults. Just as in most (all?) non-literate societies, adults perpetuate this way of helping children to come to terms with the non-human environment, even if it represents only one part of their total world view. The ideal, in the Piaget and Piaget-type studies, is that children should outgrow this approach and substitute for it a more impersonal and rational one.

A good illustration of this is an episode in the Peanuts cartoon series – again, prepared by an adult (for adults?). (This from *The Observer Review*, London, 22 March 1970, p. 43.) Charlie Brown, carrying a kite, comes to a tree, and speaks to it: 'Well! Hello, you dirty kite-eating tree! It's been a long winter, hasn't it? You look kind of hungry . . .' (The tree bares its teeth.) Charlie Brown: 'You'd like to eat this kite, wouldn't you?' (The tree's mouth curves upward, teeth still bared.) Charlie Brown: 'I hate kite-eating trees! You can starve to death for all I care!' (The tree, mouth closed and corners drooping, emits a 'Snif!') Charlie Brown: 'Go ahead and cry! I have no sympathy for you!' (The tree's mouth still droops.) Another child (Linus) comes up, takes Charlie's arm and leads him away, Charlie asking 'What are you doing? Let go of my arm! What are you doing?' (The tree's foliage is blank now – no mouth at all.) In the final scene, a girl (Lucy) sits in her little booth with a sign reading 'Psychiatric Help 5¢ . . .', speaking to Charlie Brown: 'Now let me get this straight. The person who brought you in said you were talking to a tree. . . . Is that right?'

In short, normal people don't talk to trees – except in poems (Morris's 'poetic discourse') or in allegories. Or, if they do, they don't seriously believe that *two*-way communication is possible, not in a realistically-literal fashion. At the same time, it is abundantly clear that children in Western-European-type society as well as in others, learn (are taught) a generalized kind of symbolic language which embraces plant, animal (etc.) life – and *things*. And this language is not suddenly dropped as children grow older. It continues on into adult life, although it serves different ends there – is used to convey different messages.

Cartoons and pop songs are one field where it finds expression. Cartoons are full of symbolic allusions: in political comments on war and peace, not only hawk and dove images and mythical figures like Mars or some other god of war, but also thing-symbols like war-weapons, including rockets and bombs, with quasi-human faces and sometimes the power of speech. Among pop songs, to select one example rather arbitrarily, 'Winchester Cathedral' (a 'hit' song of a few years back) illustrates the point quite well. The singer accuses the cathedral of not intervening when his (or her) sweetheart left him: 'You just stood and watched, as my baby left town . . . You could have done something, but you just didn't try . . .'

Pop songs and cartoons are on the fringe of the large and, symbolically speaking, extremely important area of poetry and drama and graphic and kinaesthetic arts. But another area of overlap in which this symbolic language is very much at home is one that is often regarded as the almost complete antithesis of the poetic and the aesthetic. This is commerce and industry – specifically, consumer advertising.

Research workers are drawn to the study of advertising for many, and quite diverse reasons. Some are involved to the point of almost complete identification with the perspective of the sellers, the agents whose business is the marketing of particular products. Psychologists have a firm foothold in this, with their professional reputation as specialists in motivation and persuasion – and resistance to persuasion. Economists too, of course. And social scientists, because this is one branch of the mass media studies we spoke about before. The social dimension is important here too: on the 'process' side, interpersonal relations, lines of influence, changes associated with upward or downward or simply spatial mobility; on the 'structural' side, status, rank, office; social class and stratification; membership of formal organizations – and so on. Advertisers may be interested in mass sales, but in the endeavour to slant their appeals more effectively they are increasingly alert to socio-cultural differentiation, and the significance of social relations and social positioning. Aspirations, beliefs, values, all come into this, from formal religious affiliation to the smallest item of behaviour or belief that could have a bearing on consumer choice.

Social scientists who participate actively in these endeavours are affiliated to specific firms, or working on problems that are of direct or indirect relevance to the industry, or to specified branches of it, e.g. within the overall range of what used to be called motivation research. Academics aside, interaction between producers and consumers is mediated, not only through interpersonal networks and so on – apparently the least stressful section of the total arena – but through advertising and other selling agents. Competition between products, and between different brands of the same kind of product, is paralleled in competition between such agents for the most lucrative advertising accounts.

Selling is 'big business'. But so is advertising. And, matching developments in the wider sphere, much more is expected of advertisers now. In this respect, a 1959 statement* is a useful summary of one point of view: it was made on the occasion of a merger between a large North American advertising agency (McCann Erickson Inc.) and a smaller Australian one (the Sydney firm of Hansen Rubensohn).

The significant change in recent years has been the decline of the adman who worked on hit-or-miss hunches and the rise of the scientific adman whose work is backed by a research team and who sees advertising as 'only a little more scientific than medicine'.

Once the adman had to have a gift for writing simple, snappy and impelling copy. ... But now you do not market a product – or you shouldn't—until you have done the maximum of market, motivation, copy, and media research. You should know that you have the right product at the right time in the right quantity at the right price with the right label, in the right package. You should know the class, age, and sex of your market, your sales and your competitors' sales over the years, your unit turnover, your share of the gross national products, and so on. You should know the personal fantasies of your purchasers, and know all about such things as Thematic Appercep- tion Tests, Rorschach Tests, Sales Conviction Tests. You should know the techniques of your media, about radio jingles, T.V. scenarios, echo mikes, props and camera angles, and you must know about their effectiveness. On top of all this the good adman is a sort of walking encyclopaedia. He should, says Mr. Bristow, of H.R.-McC. 'know the names of the latest hit tunes, how an atomic pile works, and

* P. Coleman, 'The Coming War in Advertising', *The Observer* (Australian), 31 October 1959, p. 678. A black-and-white sketch on this page shows three men in bow ties beside a wall-notice reading 'Think, Damn you, THINK!' All look harassed: and one, tossing a pill into his mouth, is clutching a sheet reading 'I dreamed I went MAD in my Maidenfor[m] Bra—'.

whether pterodactyls or Stone Age men were the first to arrive on earth'. (The worst insult you can give to an adman is to suggest that there is some tiny fragment of human nature he does not understand.) With all these facts you work out your brand image, 'the philosophy' on which you will sell (Ampol means power, Shell means security), your copy platform, the reasons why the purchaser should buy your product, and finally your whole market strategy.

Or so the adman says.

Not all of them, though. Some are depressed by the diminishing scope for individual flair and initiative, especially if that was what attracted them to the profession in the first place – the scope it seemed to offer for creativity, even if not to the same extent as in the field of 'non-commercial' art. They find teamwork uncongenial, feeling that it stifles opportunities for individual self-expression. (Actually, it can provide something resembling the Australian Aboriginal situation – individuality within a co-operative unit.) The science-versus-art bit worries some of them too. Of course, there is intermediate ground here. 'The scientific imagination', what Redfield called 'the art of social science', is just as relevant to scientific procedure as it is to art itself: a hunch about a problem that seems worth investigating, for instance. But systematic following through of that hunch, routine checking and analysis, does not necessarily attract the same people.

The new developments in advertising techniques do not please all manufacturers either. They want quick results, and for them, that is the purpose of the exercise: the research must 'pay off'.

The stress is on how to sell whatever product they happen to be concerned with at the time or, conversely, how to get people to buy it. Consumers certainly come part of the way to meet them, and certainly make demands too – but not to anything like the same extent. This is very far removed from the simple trading operations of small-scale societies, with their limited range of communications and limited range of wants. Or *is* it? In some respects, yes. We think at once of such factors as population scale, assortment of products, complexity of communications, 'cut-throat competition', 'the hard sell', and so on. As against this, however, we can think of other factors that have apparently been slower to change.

Advertising techniques are more sophisticated than they were, or so we are often told. But the kinds of appeal that they embody do not seem to have altered a great deal in the last few decades,* and comments on those appeals suggest that the same principles continue to apply. Advertisers are cautioned that, if they want to reach a 'mass' market, they must remember the facts of life: that *most* people are of no more than average intelligence and can take in only so much at one time; that the language used must be fairly elementary if the message is to 'get across'; that pictures or objects make a message easier to understand than if it is made up of words alone; that constant repetition is needed, not an appeal to logic and reason; and that emotional, not intellectual, responses are what help to sell products.

But, still within the framework of 'sell as much as possible to as many as possible' (and its counterpart of 'buy as much as possible'), the narrowing down of appeals to specialized 'publics' is reflected in the phrasing of advertisements.

The choice of verbal material has been widening. An advertiser can use colloquial everyday speech, or more formal and pedantic expressions, or words or phrases from foreign languages (i.e. foreign to the majority of readers of that particular message) or various styles of jargon, according to the potential customers he is trying to reach. Two kinds of commodity are especially conspicuous in this respect. The

* For a good summary of these points up to 1950, see D. B. Lucas and S. H. Britt, *Advertising Psychology and Research. An Introductory Book*, McGraw-Hill, 1950.

first is motor vehicles. At the prestige end of the spectrum, appeals emphasize 'quiet, aristocratic, expensive elegance'; at the other end, efficient performance – depending on the type of vehicle and the social aspirations of possible buyers. The second is clothing, and here the scope is almost limitless. All that concerns us here is the jargon employed in promoting it.

The 'young image' in men's fashions, for instance, is built around several themes. A line of suits ('the new suits') has as its slogan, 'Drop out of the father-image of the last decade'. Another advertisement, in colour, attracts attention by its block-letter shout of 'WANTED! . . . For Daring to look Different' – but goes on to reassure the reader that this is a special (actually, conforming) kind of difference: 'Enter, the confident casuals. Quietly assured. Soft-spoken. Casuals that nevertheless speak volumes for your good taste . . .' More casual still is a line of jeans-type pants (but, 'wearing Levi's is better than wearing pants'). One of a series of similar illustrations shows a pair of young people, both dressed in 'unisex' clothes but the 'girl' is recognizable as such by her slightly longer hair under a peaked cap and the fact that she is using a mirror-compact to put on lipstick; the boy rests a guitar on a duffle bag, the girl has one (knee-high) boot leaning on the high step of a stationary (goods?) train, and the caption reads: 'The pants advance./The guy can't help it. He has this thing about pants. Levi's twills. Goes berserk when he throws on the matching battle jacket. So do his girls. What a way to go.' Another in the same series features a boy on a motor-cycle with a long-haired girl behind him; the caption, 'Pack-leading pants./Drop down that gear and get into the Levi's denims. What else? A jacket that's kinda blue, too. And the deadly night shades./High rev gear. Wear them with Easyrider cool/ and you'll lay 'em in the aisles./Or where you will.' Again on the matter of jeans, a double-spread colour advertisement that combines an appeal to mothers (references to 'your boy', urging, 'give him . . .' one of these) puts this heading above a group of teenagers: 'Life wouldn't be any fun, if it wasn't for a fishing rod and his pair of jeans.'

But these appeals pale beside the opportunities that female fashions afford to advertisers, with the variables of different age-markets, rapidly changing styles, and fluctuating amounts and styles of covering, from a 'bare minimum' to full-scale formal attire with accessories. That, however, is a topic in itself, and so is the range of jargon associated with it. (E.g. a variation on the 'Just wear a smile and a Jantzen' slogan is a newspaper advertisement for a suburban boutique: 'My dears! . . . Just bring some small change and a smile. We'll supply the clothes . . .')

Not all research workers interested in the advertising field are concerned even indirectly with the 'sales and promotion' angle, except in reading selectively from reports of results (e.g. on the effectiveness of certain types of appeal as against others). Many, apparently, are simply fascinated by the nature of the content. For those who collect advertisements much as some people collect stamps, this is more than an absorbing hobby. It is also a preoccupation that advertisers would probably pander to, or encourage, as a number of them appear to do already – since one aim in advertising is to attract a potential customer's attention, as the first move in the battle, if not the most important move. (Hence the familiar, and deliberate, combination of 'pretty girls and motor cars'.)

The startle-effect or shock-effect of advertisements is limited by advertisers' codes of ethics, where these are operative, by legal sanctions, and by the possibility of public protests. In essence, many of them, apart from the straightforward 'attractive girl' eye-catcher, depend on some arresting phrase or picture, usually in combination – a mixture of verbal language and pictorial language.* Some are very simple

* J. Ruesch and W. Kees, *Nonverbal Communication* . . ., University

indeed, others more ambitious; but most rely either on the juxtaposition of items not usually found together, or on the refurbishing or alteration of the familiar in such a way that it seems unfamiliar, if not new – much as cartoons give a new twist to old stories or images. Figures of speech that have become so much a part of ordinary language that they no longer seem 'figurative', can make a different impact when they are translated into pictures. The simplest of them are affected by the same process of familiarization. The sun disc with a human face, smiling in holiday advertisements, frowning or frustrated in advertisements for air conditioning or insulation, attracts a reader's eye as a picture in contrast to words but otherwise probably passes unnoticed – because it is taken for granted as an ordinary alternative to the word 'sun' in such contexts. Similarly with moon-symbols and storm- or wind-symbols (human face with puffed cheeks, blowing).

In others, the attempt at shock-treatment is quite unsubtle. A 1970 Indian advertisement (*Illustrated Weekly of India*, Volume XCI, No. 19, 1970, p. 65) takes up most of a full page with an illustration: a man posing beside a spade, while the face of a long-haired girl, buried up to her neck in sand with the tide approaching (?), looks at him with open-mouthed admiration (?). The caption reads: 'You can get away with anything in a Bombay Dyeing suit.' And, in smaller lettering: 'The man in the Bombay Dyeing suit. Dressed to kill. Is cold-blooded about quality, ruthless about colour. Satisfies his instincts from a superb range of Wadrene ('Terene'/cotton)

---

of California Press, Berkeley, 1956, e.g. p. 30. This is a very useful overview of a topic on which it is hard to find middle-range statements between two extremes: careless but easy to read, or over-careful but unreadable. Some discussions of 'pop art', for instance, are like the more banal examples of such 'art' translated into words. See, for example, J. Rublowsky, *Pop Art, Images of the American Dream*, foreword by S. A. Green, Nelson, 1965.

and poplins – in designs and shades that will take her breath away!' Some 1969–70 Holden car dealers' advertisements do the same thing more genteelly and more obviously tongue-in-cheek. One illustration: an elderly lady and her victim, a dark-suited man writhing in pain as she triumphantly holds his arm; the caption, 'Twist a Holden dealer's arm' . . . and you will get especially advantageous treatment. Following this up, a full-length black-edged half-page spread, with text standing out in the centre: a large black heading, 'Five Salesmen Injured', and below it five names, '. . . the five top Holden salesmen in . . . have suffered serious injury to their arms caused by many arm twisting Holden buyers at . . ./However, they are still in action as they have thirty current model Holdens to sell this week . . . So hurry to . . .' (dealer's name).

A muted shock-effect is tried in a series of advertisements for a washing machine that carries the slogan, 'The Handsome Brute with the gentle touch' (a feather above the last word). One of these has a small inset picture of a Japanese woodcut, and the words, 'A Westinghouse washer will caress a priceless Japanese silk print!' The description elaborates on the strength-plus-gentleness aspect: e.g. 'To prove the point, we washed a Japanese silk print and it came up smiling "arrigato"./That's what we mean by the gentle touch./If the Westinghouse can take care of a silk print, imagine how well it looks after your delicates, from body stockings and panty hose, to petticoats, fine woollens, and even paper panties. . . .'

If the first two of these used 'offence against the person' as the basis of their pictorial appeal, the third made use of 'offence against the property'. A fourth kind emphasizes sex. For example, a 1964 Cutex 'Forbidden Fruits' lipstick advertisement urges the use of flavoured lipstick as a means of attracting, not *a* man, but several. Below a photograph of a girl with tongue slightly protruding, it adds that these 'look delicious, taste delicious . . . and so do girls who wear them.

It's a cool new way to collect men.' (The lipsticks are 'Orange Kiss', 'Peppermint Kiss', etc.)

Advertisements like these have captivated the interest of serious and not-so-serious writers – although not as many as one would expect, in view of their significance as reflection of, as well as influence on, their socio-cultural context. What does not seem to have received the same attention, although it is just as important on both of these counts, is the use of animal (etc.) and object-symbols, as in the sphere of cartoons and children's books, and so on, to convey (in this case) commercially slanted messages.

Fairy stories and nursery rhymes come into this too. To take just one example, a builder's advertisement (1963) based on the 'Three Little Pigs' theme: the lettering reads, '3 Pigs Discovered that [illustration 1] while some people build their homes with wood and straw . . . [illustration 2] and others use lightweight brick veneers . . . [illustration 3] wise people build in SOLID CLAY brick for real comfort and security.' 'All . . . homes are SOLID CLAY BRICK (not just brick and veneer)'. The first illustration shows a small pig (dark suit and tie) standing with clasped hands in the ruins of a house beside a chimney, looking pitifully at a large, slavering wolf (no clothes); the second is much the same, with only the framework of a house and some fallen bricks; in the third, a pig laughs victoriously from a window of a house (marked on the door, 'Pig 3') at a wolf lying on its back on the ground outside, puffing out little clouds of exhaustion(?).

In other cases, there is no story-line, but a direct thing-or-creature appeal.

For example, a 1970 advertisement for television sets capitalizes on current concern about programme-content with its large block-letter heading, 'Introducing Healthy Television', but the smaller lettering continues with the human analogy: '. . . Over 80% of our TVs didn't know what it was

to have a day off sick. After all, how healthy is a television . . .
that gets hot and feverish? . . .' 'Here are three healthy
specimens . . .', including a portable one that 'wears sunglasses
for outdoor viewing'. (Similarly, a newspaper feature article
on the way a television set can dominate a room illustrates
the point with a picture of 2 adults and 2 children watching a
ceiling-high set, its eyes looking out from the screen and its
mouth, curving between the two adjuster-knobs, shouting
'Look at me!!') One refrigerator is advertised (1970) as 'The
refrigerator that knows all about women'. Another, 'The
Refrigerator that speaks for itself', made a personal press
appeal (1957) in cursive hand-written script: '*To your husband
and you.*/You are invited to phone . . ., and make a date with
me./Even if the Refrigerator you are using is only 12 months
old, you will probably find I'll do much more for you, and
save you money./You may see me on display in the Showroom
of . . . at . . .' And, on another occasion, '*It's Easy – and it
pays you*/to have me in your kitchen./Users say they have
never seen any Refrigerator more beautiful, or more capable,
or more easily obtainable./You simply can't believe it until
you see me, and hear my story. I'm right out in front at . . .
and I speak for myself./Leonard.'

An enormous range of objects and creatures is personified in
this way, in words or pictures or both. A 'happy house', safe
from the extremes of hot or cold, has a smiling face; an 'in-
secure' house looks anxious. In advertisements for pesticides,
moths and silverfish and other pests carry placards reading
'Unfair to moths' (etc.); and snails with masks and hats pulled
low over their eyes, and carrying guns, tell other snails, 'This
is a hold-up – we've got to get out of here!' Cheerful-faced
pigs declare that so-and-so's brand of bacon is best. A lawn
food claims that it 'makes lawns sit up and sing' – and a
human-shaped piece of lawn is shown doing just that, holding
a flower in one hand. Illustrating a bath-salts cure for 'burning

feet', the soles of two feet, with anguished faces, are surrounded by flames. In a long series of small advertisements for CBS Coronet Records (middle 1950s), a personified record with arms, legs and a coronet, has some varied experiences that are co-ordinated with the records he is promoting: e.g. for 'Lola's Theme' from 'Trapeze' (1957), as a girl dives from one trapeze bar high above a circus ring, he sits on the other reading a book labelled 'Les Girls'. In another long series, also in the middle 1950s, a partly-humanized tractor named 'Fergie' acts as a spokesman for his firm. In one, wearing his usual tam-o-shanter, he 'has other tractors crying for mercy!' – and this is graphically illustrated; in another, under the main caption, 'Here's the Ferguson Answer to Low Cost Fodder Conservation', he wears a mortar board and holds a Quiz sheet in his two front 'hands' (tyres) while he beams benignly over his glasses at two smaller, human figures in trousers and shirtsleeves – and upturned hats (i.e., presumably, working farmers *plus* others). If things need mending or sealing with sticky tape, 'A Little Bear' will fix it. And if people forget, Kodak says (December 1969), 'Pictures remember': 'Give the gift that remembers in colour'.

But cars, especially, lend themselves to such treatment. They move, they emit sounds; and whether or not they are extensions of their owner's 'ego', they are almost members of a household, and almost household pets. A Volkswagen advertisement is quite prosaic, as far as symbolic statements go, and so are its illustrations, but its text has a hint of something more: 'The 1970 Volkswagen Fastback goes think-think instead of chug-chug.' It continues in conventional terms, explaining, 'Because it's run by a computer instead of carburettors./No kidding, an actual computer. A little black box we call "the brains".' It ends on the human-analogy note, however: 'Volkswagen has always been a thinking man's car./ Now you just have to decide if you're the thinking car's man.'

Other advertisements (1969–70) urge readers to 'Have a love affair with a Fiat', and at least one used-car dealer has followed this up with his own appeal (1970): above a large itemized sheet of vehicles-for-sale, a large heart shape encloses the head and shoulders of a young man and woman, kissing; the caption surrounding them reads, 'You can't have an Italian love affair with these cars/as they aren't Fiats! but with these other makes you can have a ball! . . .'

Some of the best advertisements, however, from this point of view, are petrol-promoters, with cars merely as petrol-consumers: the car-type itself does not signify. A 1970 Esso example in the London *Observer* is headed, 'We say motor oil should get up quicker in the morning'. The text begins, 'When you put your car to bed for the night, the oil that lubricates the engine drains back into the oil reservoir./So when you start the engine in the morning, the oil's a little slow to get circulating again properly. (The colder the morning, the slower it is.)' . . . The main illustration: a portly gentleman, bowler-hatted and carrying a brief case, is looking ostentatiously at his watch, and at a car that is slumped sideways against a garage wall, looking blearily back at him. Another fuel-series (middle 1950s) sponsored Energol, 'the Oiliest Oil' ('Recommended by Rolls-Royce'): in each of these, a small car (different makes, and with slightly different faces) is pictured smiling appreciatively as a neatly dressed man in a suit and tie presents it with a bouquet of flowers, rolls out a carpet for it, flicks it carefully with a feather duster, holds an umbrella over it in a rain shower, or (a square, rather elderly-looking car; a man with dark coat and pin-stripe trousers, balding head with bristly white moustache and eyebrows) brings it a labelled bottle and a champagne glass on a tray. The caption in each case is, 'If you really care for your car/always use Energol . . .'

A 1960–62 Shell series had even more graphic illustrations,

accompanied by their principal slogan of 'Cars love Shell' (the name 'Shell' enclosed in a scallop-shell design, the firm's main emblem). The earliest showed a single, smiling car in a landscape while the text explained, '. . . and with good reason. They know they can't get lost, can't knock themselves out on bad roads, when there's a Shell map . . . to guide them. They appreciate Shell's detailed lists of motel . . . locations, too. . . . No wonder cars and drivers, too, love Shell's Touring Service . . .'. Or, still smiling, a car looks up at a Shell petrol pump and a couple of little hearts float in the air above it: the text below the main heading, '. . . because it makes them feel so good./So give *your* car its heart's desire. Introduce it to Shell – you'll find they were meant for each other.' Another, a high-backed car with long curved eyelashes and an open, bow-shaped mouth: heading, 'How to Live to 100,000 or Longer'; text, 'She's a beautiful bus! . . . a stately lady from '28. Since the day she "came out" and drew toots from admirers, she's been in love . . . with Shell. *Every thousand miles she's had a lift* – on a Shellubrication hoist – something every old lady and sprightly young miss of a motor car should do to keep in perfect shape! And there's a lot of life in the old girl yet./Her secret? Sh! Sh! Sh! Sh! Shellubrication'. Large letters, 'Cars love Shellubrication'. Others in the series showed cars, hearts fluttering around them, riding in Shell transport-vehicles or cuddled up to them – in one case, a ship with eye and open mouth in profile, looking down at it. A sub-series featured photographs of animal, etc., pairs, plus the car-Shell pair: two dogs sitting together, nuzzling each other – two dog-faced cars nuzzling each other in front of a Shell emblem; two fish nuzzling each other in a bowl – two fish-shaped cars doing the same; two budgerigars on a perch . . . – two bird-shaped cars, also on a perch; a giraffe nuzzling her (?) young – A Shell pump with long hose bending over toward a little car that rises eagerly up to meet it; a koala mother nursing its baby – a Shell pump with human face, and a baby-faced car nestling in its arms. All of these repeat that 'Cars love Shell because' . . . it 'is the petrol that does cars good . . . and cars seem to know it'. But some of them, too, add an oblique reminder that the analogy is not to be taken literally: cars love Shell 'because, like living things, they respond to the way they are treated.'

Like living things – but not, themselves, living: symbolic representations, like the Shell emblem or badge, not to be taken literally. As a (1968–9) tyre retread advertisement put it, under a prominent black heading in a full-page spread, 'The retread fairytale': 'Once upon a time . . . a lot of things said about retreads sounded like a fairytale./Many people still would have you believe in retread fairytales. For instance, you might get the impression retreads are like new tyres. . . ./Like all good fairytales, these stories should not be taken seriously.' A different kind of advertisement, for du Pont & Co. of Wall Street (*New York Times*, 18 April 1965), uses the word 'fable' in presenting the message. Under the heading, 'Fables for the Very Rich/(and those who would like to be)', an owl in tails, waistcoat and bow tie, with cane and top hat on the ground behind him, holds in one hand a book marked 'Budget' and in the other, feather-end thoughtfully under his nose (beak), a quill pen. The text reads: 'The Owl and His Budget./A night Owl, rebuked by his wife for his wild spending, decided to go on a budget. Asked if his budget helped him save any money he replied, "Sure does. By the time I balance it every night it's too late to go anywhere"./Moral: money doesn't grow on sprees.' The message continues: 'No, nor on hopes, either. Folks who like to conserve money usually do something about it. Like investing part of their income in tax-free municipals' (etc.).

The truth–falsity issue applies just as much to advertisements as to myth, and these too have implications for action.

The warning, *caveat emptor*, is just as relevant in this large-scale commercial world as it is in any dealings with fair-ground salesmen. The language the advertisements employ must be read on different levels: and it is a language that children begin to learn while they are still too young to read it for themselves. Some of the same imagery, verbal and pictorial, persists into, and throughout, adult life.

The illustration for a (1970) refrigerator advertisement could come almost straight from a young child's comic book of the more innocuous sort – which is why some adults dismiss this kind of pictorial appeal as 'childish'. The caption (large block letters): 'Westinghouse Keeps its Cool and Banishes Frost . . . Forever!' The illustration: a Batman-style figure, high boots and long gloves, cape billowing behind him, determined expression, thrusts forward a huge clenched fist bearing the words (block letters, in white) 'The End of the Ice Age', dispersing, in a dripping cloud, three little frost-creatures who shake their arms in despair: 'Westinghouse Super-Cool Dry-Freezes Hoary Frost and the Messy-Drip Gang!' Less obviously childish, a car-dealer's (1970) advertisement shows a childbirth scene: a woman in bed, hospital equipment around, and surgical instruments and bowls in the foreground; three white-masked and -gloved attendants, one holding a naked baby upside down; and the caption, 'We won't deliver your new Valiant quite like this but we will take as much care.' And, still pursuing the 'baby' analogy, the firm claims that it makes 'a serious attempt to eliminate teething problems *before* delivery'.

The illustrative content in each of these is very different, but they belong within the same category of figurative language, one that is taken with a mixture of belief and non-belief, credulity and cynicism. The amount and nature of the figurative content varies. In some instances it is minimal, and the appeal does not hedge – as in a washing machine advertisement directed at husbands (and wives): 'The wife this saves may be your own!' Appeals to adults via children can be mixed, too: like the photograph of a baby, too young to talk yet, ostensibly warning his mother that he'll stage a protest if she doesn't get him the right brand of baby powder. And so are appeals to children. In the breakfast cereal field, the mixture is exemplified in the different types of pictorial appeal and thing-appeal that come with various packets at various times. The range here is from 'space-age' toys, little plastic rockets and other machines that need careful assembling, through puzzles and riddles and pictures-for-painting, to illustrated appeals such as 'Tony Tiger says . . .' and small plastic anthropomorphic creatures of all types in a variety of colours (e.g. 'vegetable sports', vegetables with arms, legs and faces, like Spudsy Boxer and Runner Bean, taking part in a sporting contest; King Nep-tune and his Sea-weeders, in an under-water orchestra, including Fanny Fantail the singer and other fish – and so on).

The deliberate 'invention' or presentation of personified images of animated objects and plants is part of a series of campaigns in which the seller or his agent is trying to evoke a favourable response to a particular product. But as in the case of cartoons, comic strips, travel posters and similar media, it is also part of a well-established tradition in which this kind of appeal is both legitimate and acceptable. The scale on which it takes place and the purposes for which it is designed, and the shifting nature of the images, have no direct counterparts in most non-literate societies – or probably in most non-European societies, for that matter. With increasing industrialization and the intensifying of popular commercial appeals, we could even speak of a corresponding increase in animation and personification.

These appeals go well beyond the level of satisfying basic needs, the needs that must be met if a human being is to survive as a physical organism. But the line between 'needs' and 'wants' is never sharply drawn – as Malinowski found, in his classic attempt to differentiate between basic and derived needs. To Aboriginal Australians, coloured ochres and ceremonial decorations were not luxuries but necessities, just as birds' feathers and decorative leaves were to the eastern New Guinea highlanders. The psycho-emotional aspect of culturally defined needs is a force to be reckoned with in all human societies. It is merely that, in our own, this force has been deliberately nurtured and expanded. That objects should play so large a part in it is not surprising, since Western societies are more thing-oriented than most: people manipulate others through objects, as one facet of the world of people manipulating objects. If we were to speak of rationality and non-rationality here, we could say that commercial advertising represents rational manipulation of other people's irrationality, insofar as it rests on appeals through emotion rather than through reason. But while all societies show this mixture (of emotion and reasoning), in the economic sphere as in others, the fundamental core of techniques and information and skills in all of them is realistic and practical, in premises or means–end procedures or both. The realm of the non-empirical, of magic and religion, impinges on it through increase rites, prayers for rain and for harvest, blessing of fishing fleets and taxi-cabs, and similar manifestations. This is not necessarily confined to organized, institutionalized religious beliefs and rites. And another point should be borne in mind here. It is one thing to identify a phenomenon like myth or mythical thinking, as something that appears to be present in every human society to date: it is another to claim (as Malinowski did for myth) that every society *needs* this. That may possibly be so, but moving from an 'is' to an 'ought' means moving more obviously from description to evaluation.

In Western European-type society, religion has become much more sharply separated from other spheres of living than it was, traditionally, in Aboriginal Australia or in New Guinea. In the first place, membership in a community of believers, or worshippers, is now a more selective matter. It rests to a much larger extent on individual choice and decision. It is not taken for granted as an inevitable concomitant of belonging to a particular society or a particular social unit or social stratum (or class). In the second place, the beliefs and actions that go with it are not diffused through the whole field of behaviour and ideas but only through certain parts of it. This has been referred to as the trend toward secularization, although there are also suggestions of a counter-trend toward sanctification.* However, to a much greater degree than in Aboriginal Australia, and to some extent more than in New Guinea, we can speak of a range of relatively secular activity and ideas, formally distinguishable from the sphere of religious and mythical thought. And consumer advertising is usually regarded as one facet of this.

The claim has been made that, in our kind of society, many of the issues which have troubled non-industrial man are no longer so important – as in Ellul's reference to the *new* mythology as dealing, not with the creation of man, but with the creation of the machine. Machines can certainly give an appearance of movement, of life such as man shares with other living beings in contrast to the inanimate world. Animation of images in advertising is comparable to animation of machines: it is mechanical, it can be switched on and off by man.

But whether or not we speak of formal, institutionalized religious commitment, we can make some sort of distinction between the realm of religion or the supernatural, the world which man may believe he can influence up to a point but for which he is not wholly responsible, and the more or less secular sphere in which events are taken to rest on human

* E.g. R. Merton, *Social Theory and Social Structure*, Free Press, Glencoe, 1957, pp. 547–60.

actions and decisions. 'Animation' in Marett's* sense was a feature of tribal or, as he called it, 'primitive' religion: the inanimate world was supposedly independent of the actions or will of human beings, but 'on the face of it', this might 'be no more than a simple straightforward act of personification'. In advertising, we could use the same word in a different sense, with this meaning of personification or anthropomorphism: the attribution of human or personal qualities to non-human creatures or objects. But the power that animates these images in the symbolic world of cartoons and advertising is human power – the attempted manipulation of persons by other persons, or the attempts of persons to influence or amuse or entertain others, through the symbolism of objects and creatures in quasi-human form. And in many cases this means framing in personal terms a relationship that is, essentially, impersonal. Robin Williams has referred to this mixed kind of action as pseudo-Gesellschaft. Others have spoken of it as pseudo-Gemeinschaft, a process in which the form of the appeal attempts to disguise the manipulative intent by evoking a response characteristic of a Gemeinschaft-type situation – a warm, friendly, personal one. McLuhan† has suggested that advertising is moving away from the impersonal 'mass' approach toward 'a more personalized service': and he uses the word 'retribalism' for this new, more personal relationship. Other social and demographic factors, however, would seem to militate against that.

Mythology and religion are concerned with establishing man's place in nature and the universe and his relations with other men, with uniting and differentiating men on the basis of shared belief and shared activity. Personification, like other 'symbolic language', extends into the commercial world in

* *The Threshold of Religion*, Methuen, 1909/14, pp. xxxii, 6–7, 14.

† In a talk in 1966 in New York, reported by I. Merson, 'Research in Review', *Journal of Advertising Research*, Vol. 7, 1967, pp. 54–5.

which advertising is one kind of communication between one set of people and another: would-be sellers and potential buyers. There is no *common* action, although we can speak of interdependence within an economic system.

Personification is a neutral term, that tells us nothing of the context in which it is used. It is at home in the sphere of religion and myth, *and* in what is sometimes taken to be the direct opposite of that – the sphere of commerce and business, the market-place as against the church. But although this commercial approach to the non-human world is fairly sophisticated and deliberately manipulative, secular as contrasted with sacred, the form that it takes is an example of mythical thinking: and mythical thinking, like the metaphorical use of verbal language, relies on analogies and emotional cause-and-effect connections rather than on systematic testing and exploration. In this sense, it is often cited as hindering the development of discursive, objective scientific thought – although it need not do so, if it is kept within bounds. There is a world of difference between the poetic use of symbolic language in a self-conscious, or relatively self-conscious, way, and the emotionally charged belief that is an accepted characteristic of myth.

Nevertheless, consumer advertising is one arena in which these differing perspectives meet, as they do in the less obviously competitive field of comic strips and political cartoons. The figurative and symbolic images of poetry, the traditional and quasi-traditional themes of myth, folktale and fairytale, are well established in human socio-cultural living. In one sense, technology and 'material objects as commodities' are accommodated to this framework. And all of these are mutually reinforcing. Despite the fact that their localized forms and expressions are not mutually intelligible without a process of translation and interpretation, like separate 'dialects', these themes and images appear to be no less significant than they used to be, as a fundamental human 'language'.

10

Prophets and Other People

A 1967 Editorial in the *Journal of Advertising Research*, entitled 'Why Prophecy Fails',* contrasts prediction with prophecy – the first depending for its success on accuracy, the second on 'uncertainty reduction'. Science is 'the prediction business'. 'Prophets are in demand as television entertainers, advisers to government, university professors and long-range planners in business' – and in advertising, too, described as 'an especially uncertain arm of business' and therefore sadly in need of them. A cynic might suggest that the obverse of this applies as far as potential consumers are concerned: i.e. that the aim in that case is uncertainty stimulation, as a means of prodding customers into discontent with what they have so they will turn to something new, or something more than they have already.

Of course, there are exceptions, and among them are 'security merchants' such as insurance firms. But what kind of security? Here is a 1970 example, caption in large white letters on a black ground with an inset head-and-shoulders photograph of a man and woman arguing: 'Love doesn't always find a way.' The text, in smaller lettering (italics added): 'Love is a word you hear a lot today. If you take in all the pop song words, then "love" is the gospel according to youth./Unfortunately song writers are often wrong, love isn't much use

* Vol. 7, No. 1, 1967, p. 64; by C. K. Ramond.

at the supermarket check-out on Saturday morning. Love won't pay the water-rates or dentist bills or hire purchase. *Money is what you need.*/And when you have money problems, you often get love problems. Nothing turns off the magic quicker than money worries./Most marriages need a pattern to build in security. Insurance is nearly always part of that pattern. A.M.P. insurance . . ./Why don't you talk with an A.M.P. man? He'll build a plan for you that you can handle easily. Your money will grow little by little *until you have real security built into your lives* . . ./A.M.P. insurance is security./ Security can be very, very romantic.'

'Money is what you need.' Not all advertisements put it as bluntly as this, or state so frankly that it is money, not love, which makes the world go round. But it is at least latent in many of them, to the extent that advertisers and the manufacturers and others who sponsor them have been labelled 'prophets of materialism'.

A few years ago, Toynbee, visiting the United States, is reported (in 1961) to have said that 'Madison Avenue represents a greater threat to Western civilization than Communism': 'I would suggest that the destiny of our Western civilization turns on the issue of our struggle with Madison Avenue even more than it turns on the issue of our struggle with Communism.' Perhaps he was referring to U.S.-style advertising rather than to advertising in general – the press report does not make this clear.

Advertising, of course, covers many different facets. We need not go into its history, which has been quite well documented. But one facet that has a bearing on cross-cultural contacts, if not cross-cultural communication, is tourism – the stepping-up of first-hand contacts by visitors to other countries – and its converse, the bringing of foreign goods and ideas to people on their own home ground.

As travel to other lands becomes easier, however, travel to 'unknown lands' becomes correspondingly harder. Few places remain remote and inaccessible, apart from a diminishing number of mountain tops and underwater retreats, and what were once relatively – *relatively*: never entirely – isolated cultures have been changing accordingly. Tourists who look for something exotic and different may find it; but it is likely to be slanted in response to their demands and expectations as well as to other outside influences, whether they see it from the vantage point of familiar comforts (an almost-anonymous hotel-culture setting) or attempt to merge into it, hippy-style.

On the other hand, people can travel vicariously, in time as well as in space. Where Marco Polo saw at first hand the Chinese city of Hangchow ('it is without doubt the finest and most splendid city in the world'),* we can read about it in rich detail at second hand, as depicted by social historians like Jacques Gernet.† And the volume of material on contemporary and near-contemporary societies, including the non-literate, tribal world, is already formidable and continuing to grow. Much of it is serious, attempting to provide a truthful and un-biased account of other (and similar) ways of life.

Some of it, however, is designed to cater for consumers who want something other than that – mass media effects in Mondo Cane style, for instance. Cinema advertisements are notorious in this respect. (E.g. illustrations of 'topless' girls with captions to match: 'Africa Sexy', '1st release! Native Nakedness. Striptease . . . Ritual Dances from the Hot Spots of Africa!' And 'Karamoja, land of the naked people. Stark Naked People! Indescribable – unbelievable! See Weird, Revolting Customs Conceived 6,000 Years Ago – In Living

* *The Travels . . .*, trans. by R. E. Latham, pp. 184–202; he called it 'Kinsai'.

† *Daily Life in China on the Eve of the Mongol Invasion, 1250–1276,* Allen and Unwin (Ruskin House), 1962, trans. by H. M. Wright. (French ed. 1959, Hachette, Paris.) He discusses, also, Chinese relations with 'barbarians', including the Mongols.

Colour. Raw Fact . . . A Thousand Times Stranger than Fiction!' 'Plus: Hell Kitten – The story of a teenage tigress'.) Paperbacks and magazines cater for the same, apparently insatiable, demand. 'Exotic' foods are taken almost for granted – not only once-foreign commodities that have become acclimatized to their new environment, but more deliberately exotic items like tinned baby bees and chocolate ants and bears' livers. New drugs-of-addiction (or dependence) have made more of an impact. Marihuana has taken its place alongside alcoholic drinks as far as actual consumption goes, even in countries (like Australia) where its use has not been legalized despite strong pressures in favour of doing so. But sex, nudity and violence, separately or in combination, represent areas of special interest to the mass media and, in one way or another, to people in general. They have pan-human relevance, but they take on various guises in particular socio-cultural settings: and these different guises, these variations on familiar themes, provide additional growing points of socio-cultural change.

In a society that is accustomed to clothing, public or semi-public nudity can be exciting, whether the clothing is only a shredded bark skirt (as in the New Guinea highlands) or something more voluminous. Controversies about 'topless' waitresses, dancers and so on have not exactly died down, but they have merged into the fields of fashion and theatrical drama. Forecasts that clothing will be abandoned altogether, not merely occasionally, usually locate this possibility in the distant future – like a United States designer who claimed, in 1966, that in about 100,000 years people would be able to rub themselves with a heat-controlling chemical substance, choosing 'golden glow' or green or blue or pink, whichever they wanted. (According to press reports, a 1970 'Miss Nude America' contest was held at Naked City, a nudist resort in Indiana, with a 'Mr Nude America' contest to follow in 1971.)

Contemporary fashion designers have been quick to seize on the possibilities of changing ideas on nudity, or near-nudity, especially as regards females, because it allows them greater play along the continuum from almost complete cover-up (with maxi-skirts and trouser suits, and even something resembling a yashmak) to see-through clothing and brief bikinis. And, of course, advertisers or other agents in the so-called promotion mix have capitalized on it too – especially in 'underfashions', which receive far more consistent, year-round attention in the mass media than swim-suits do. Three 1969–70 examples illustrate this nicely. The first: a full page spread, mostly taken up with a photograph of a kneeling, long-haired girl, no obvious topcovering, small photograph of a dark-suited man at one side; large heading, 'Skin's In!'; the text continues, 'says Leon Worth. Wear it. Bare it. Skin's In! A wild no-colour colour that goes with everything! . . . Stampede with Leon's Girls to his nearest Leon Worth Panti-Hose bar. Get the freedom of Skin – in all five Worth Nova panti-hose . . .' The second, Berlei, with variant sub-captions ('We know how a woman wants to feel!' and 'Be one of the Beautiful People in Berlei'): 'Berlei brings you the next best thing to bare. The body bra. . . . You'll look like you're not wearing a bra at all but you'll feel sensational'; an alternative to this. '. . . (the closest thing to you yet.) Low in front. Silky soft. Very sexy. It's shaped to bare you up. Fit like a second skin. A great bra to be seen in under see-throughs. . . .'; another, in large caption, 'Even nice girls like to feel nude'; and in small lettering, 'Just how far can a nice girl go these days? The answer is our body bra. It lets you feel nude in the nicest possible way./So do our Pretty Naturals. The briefest, barest briefs ever. Bare yourself in natural, blue, pink, black or white. . . .' The third example: full page spread, large photograph of a kneeling long-haired girl, no obvious top-covering, beside a large caption, 'feel naked for 99c'; and in smaller lettering, 'only Genevieve offers the blissful "naked feel" of absolute freedom in panty hose. . . .'

This is artifice almost meeting nature, but not quite: the customer is a 'Nature Girl', as a fourth advertisement put it, but not *entirely* natural. It purports to offer 'the best of both worlds' – to the manufacturer, for whom consistent, 'free' nudity (as in the Australian Aboriginal situation, traditionally) would be a commercial disaster; and to the customer, who is able to enjoy the feeling of nudity without some of its disadvantages: the simulated variety is respectable, and *improves* on nature. In fact, this is the 'respectable fringe' of a world in which conventional middle-class values have been increasingly and conspicuously called in question and, often, dramatically rejected.

On one hand, the borderline between nature and artifice, 'fact' and 'fiction', is becoming more blurred – as in some pop art, which deliberately glorifies the mundane and the vulgar (as it would once have been called). There is strong, though probably still minority, support for the principle that art (fiction, drama, etc.) should not only reflect real life, but also reproduce real life: for example, that sex-on-the-stage or on the screen should not be simply hinted at or represented symbolically, but should be an actual performance.

Views on sexual normality differ, and so do responses to material of various kinds (verbal, graphic, etc.) which is regarded as falling outside that range. Nevertheless, only so many permutations are possible. Granted that putting a particular action into a different context gives it a different flavour or a different quality, such as transferring an action usually defined as private into a setting defined as public or semi-public, the possibilities are not inexhaustible. That applies to both 'influence' and 'reflection' – the portrayal or interpretation of what to do, how to do it, what other people (of various types) are doing. And it has been suggested that sex in this public-entertainment sense 'will be a bore' by the mid 1970s. But once the principle of complete enactment instead of simulation is accepted, as the core of a dramatic event, it need not be confined to sex. And there are plenty of precedents of 'real live' drama in this sense, from gladiators to bull fights, not excluding the occasional small spectacles in the New Guinea highlands where a man taken in battle was publicly, and slowly, hacked to death. Linton* once emphasized man's 'capacity for being bored', which he saw as being partly responsible for basic inventions. But it finds other outlets too, such as demands for recreation and entertainment: and again the mass media, in the shape of press and cinema advertisements, take up the theme, for example in promoting the film 'Hard Contract': 'What do the beautiful people do when they've done everything?/They've taken the next chilling step in human experience./It has to do with killing.'

These pressures for live performances, for thrills at first hand, are part of a more pervasive demand for a truly permissive society. This contends, in effect, that nothing should be closed to anyone, that nobody should be in a position to dictate to anyone else, that a person should be allowed to 'do his own thing' in his own way without interference. The slogan, 'Anything goes', is taken up as a cliché to suit the occasion, and the field of clothing fashions is sometimes assumed to reflect a wider state of affairs – as in this press feature on 'Anarchy in Fashion'†: '. . . the point is that anything goes – and anything comes from anywhere . . . /What it all adds up to is total fashion anarchy.' '. . . the thing has once again become a matter of personal taste.'/'It's simply that the lack of rules on clothes reflects the lack of rules anywhere else; and this bit, at least, is one that we can enjoy.'

Not so long ago, many Europeans took a stand of superiority on the matter of clothes, mocking at tribal people and other

---

* *Study of Man*, p. 90.

† K. Whitehorn, in *The Observer Review*, 18 January 1970, p. 30.

non-Europeans for not being able to wear them properly, not knowing how to co-ordinate their garments – or going without any. Now, however, fashion illustrations and displays include what many Europeans – and others – regard as preposterous clothing, as well as self-conscious and not entirely successful attempts to appear nude or almost-nude without seeming unnatural.

Not so long ago, anthropologists were going to some lengths to dispel the idea that tribal peoples had no rules, to show that the social order which prevailed in those societies was no less real and effective for all that it was framed in an unfamiliar idiom. Now, however, if some writers are to be believed, it is almost as if the tables have been turned. To Toynbee, of course, what is happening in Western societies today is simply a sign of the barbarization of European civilization by the 'outer proletariat' – Africans, American Indians and the like. But, whether we take 'barbarization' in the original, more neutral sense ('barbarian' as indicating merely differences in language and culture) or as having a derogatory connotation, we could just as well say that this has been the fate of peoples who were overtaken by one manifestation or another of the cultures of Western Europe. And the same argument applies in their case as in the case of Europeans themselves: are technical achievements enough? What other benefits has civilization taught? And, again, what is civilization?

The question, What is civilization?, has not been far away throughout this discussion, even though we have been focusing on other topics. It has in fact been latent in all of them, in the various facets we mentioned before – quality of living, consideration for other people, relations with outsiders, material and economic achievements, and so on. But now we need to look at it again.

Some social scientists prefer to speak of modernization. There is perhaps a division here, although a fuzzy-edged one, between archaeologists, art-historians and other past-oriented or conservative scholars on one hand, and future-oriented scholars (and others) such as economists. At least, anyone writing seriously about civilization seems impelled to deal with the past as much as with the present and future, paying lip-service, if nothing more, to what has been said about earlier 'civilizations'. In dealing with modernization, however, this is more often sidestepped – unless the writer is using the concept specifically in relation to some empirical situation in the past; but in any event, he need not confine his attention to what have been called 'civilizations'.

'Modernization' usually seems to imply extension and intensification of most or all of these features:* networks of interaction between persons, social and spatial mobility, circulation of goods and services (including employment, and division of labour), urban-centredness, literacy, secularization, scientific perspective, mass communication, bureaucratic organization, intra-national control and supra-national relations – and, not least, an orientation toward change. These are familiar items, not too different from what has often been said about 'civilization'. But the overall impact *is* different, or different in its emphasis. The stress seems to be on economic growth, a label that is sometimes used as an alternative to modernization, and on questioning of the established order. And the impression it conveys is, quite often, more that of an *un*civilizing process.

One possible distinction, then, is between civilization as a state and modernization as a process. It is true that writers on

* See, for example, K. Biggerstaff, 'Modernization – and Early Modern China', *Journal of Asian Studies*, Vol. XXV, No. 4, 1966, p. 609. He lists and discusses criteria proposed by a Conference on Modern Japan, meeting at Hakone in 1960, and reported on by J. W. Hall in *Changing Japanese Attitudes Toward Modernization* (M. B. Jansen, ed., Princeton University Press, 1965). Biggerstaff adds (p. 610) 'a substantial per capita increase in capital', and the need to consider changes in values.

civilization mostly see it, not only as an outcome of change, but also as a series of continuing adaptations to external and internal pressures (Kroeber's and Toynbee's challenge-and-response) which it must make if it is to survive. Most of them, however, also use the word as a substantive – a civilization, civilizations – implying a condition that can be, and has been, achieved: a goal or end, rather than a means. Toynbee went so far as to claim* that this goal of civilization has never actually been reached, except perhaps by a few individual persons. Nevertheless, he does not hesitate to write about 'civilizations' in the substantive sense.

Modernization is a more open-ended idea, embodying the aspect of change as such, rather than some possible or desirable end-product of change. And, for a number of writers,† protest of one kind or another is an inherent and inevitable feature of it. Social eruptions and breakdown, anomie (lack of consensus, uncertainty, inability to predict other people's likely responses, failure to agree on the norms appropriate to a given situation, etc.), and even chaos, may be seen as the almost inevitable prelude to a more stable and coherent social order. And although 'modernization' is not a neutral term – a society that is going through this process is, in current jargon, 'with it', not backward or 'traditional' – the quality of human living that it entails is not necessarily seen as being good in itself. Nor is the outcome. The process may turn out to be unmanageable. A society may be unable to adjust its orientation to the actuality, or even the idea, of a succession of unanticipated changes from outside or from within its own boundaries; and, in an interlocking world, breakdown in one can have cumulative effects in the international sphere.

Other factors are involved, too.

* *Civilization on Trial*, p. 55.
† E.g. S. N. Eisenstadt, *Modernization: Protest and Change*, Prentice-Hall, Englewood Cliffs, N.J., 1966.

News items and features articles in the mass media, speakers at conferences, and so on, vie with one another in dwelling on the inevitability of drastic change and the possibility, even probability, of destruction of human life and property on a hitherto undreamt-of scale, and maybe *in toto* – if not through deliberate malice or intent, then as a kind of by-product.

Some reports highlight the possibility of a sudden catastrophe, one that strikes with little or no prior warning – an atomic or nuclear explosion, a major earthquake triggered off by underground storage of potentially active waste matter, somebody pushing the wrong button by mistake or the 'right' button in a moment of panic or setting in motion some fatal but irreversible train of events in the course of a partly-understood experiment.

Others warn of equally alarming and more surely inevitable disasters now in the process of development. Chemical and faecal and oil contamination of water and food supplies (press report: 'Most of World's Water Impure'). Air pollution in industrial zones and in cities where motor traffic presents other problems too, e.g. of road congestion and of increasing accident rates. 'Noise pollution', including the problem of adapting to ordinary jet as well as supersonic 'planes. Large-scale erosion, as in areas of extensive mining development, deforestation, or over-grazing. Shortage of food and living space in proportion to the steep growth in the world's population. The problem of disposing of a mounting accumulation of 'virtually indisposable' industrial and domestic waste. Increased consumption of drugs of dependence. And the possibility of rising ocean-levels following the melting of the polar ice-cap (an unplanned 'side-effect'), inundating the majority of the world's largest cities.

Other press headlines continue the themes. 'Science Fiction comes True' (1970; outline of technical developments previously regarded as impossible and almost incredible).

'Nightmare Society Predicted' (1969; Salvador Luria's prediction that 'man can be repaired or manufactured until he becomes a robot'). 'Nuclear Pile-up is Worrying Leaders' (1969: British–U.S. talks on the urgent need for international arms control and limitation in 'this alarming situation'). 'Professor: Ice age may come' (1969; through global pollution resulting from over-population, blotting out the sun). 'Scientist: Stop the world at 2,000m. (1969; otherwise over-population will doom the earth to a million years of war, misery and chaos, with only occasional interludes of peace). 'Report hints at births out of control' (1969, 1970; report by U.N. population commission). 'Warning of a Wobbling World', 'Expert Opposes U.S., Soviet Plans. Warns on dangers if rivers turned inland' (1970; reports from a UNSSCO-sponsored conference in Paris, warning of 'unpredictable and possibly disastrous consequences' if the flow of major rivers in the northern hemisphere were reversed: 'We cannot predict what will happen under man's influence, when we don't even know what is happening in nature'). 'Pacific Ocean is Falling Apart' (1970; 'gravity is pulling its seabed apart', and Hawaii would eventually 'disappear in the deep Japan trench'). 'Australia could split in two, he says' (1968; a 1954 earthquake in South Australia 'was a modern-day sign' that this could be happening). 'U Thant: Ten years to solve problems' (1969; otherwise they 'will have reached such staggering proportions that they will be beyond our power to control'). 'Uranium Warning' (1970; plans for wider production of enriched uranium, ostensibly for commercial use but with atomic implications). 'Disaster seen for London in plans' (1969; criticism of traffic and road features of the Greater London Development Plan, as 'a blueprint for disaster'). 'War Germs Destruction will be a Big Problem' (1969; U.S. concern about what to do with 'millions of chemical bombs and canisters of man-made diseases', now that these have been officially renounced as weapons of war). 'More listen to theory on World decay (Ehrlich, author of *The Population Bomb*, preaching a 'message of mankind's impending doom', 'has become a trend-setter'; 1969).

General warnings include book review headings such as 'Pollution is poisoning man, say scientists' (1969; and a prediction 'that humanity will be extinct by the year 2064'), 'Nature, destroyed in the name of progress' (1969; 'Man's conquest of nature is nearing its goal – the almost total destruction of the natural environment'), 'The price of progress is reaping a big debt' (1969; the need for 'conservation of fauna, flora and natural areas'), 'All in the name of progress' (1969; a proposal 'that a small nuclear device be detonated on the moon to find out what it is made of'; earlier in that year, another U.S. suggestion was 'that one of the two moons which orbit Mars' could be blasted out of its present orbit and 'brought back to earth for study'), and 'Pollution is prompting some bleak forecasts' (1969, 1970; e.g. that 'the world's oceans will be lifeless before the end of the century unless pollution is checked', 'Man's Destruction' (1970; 'Man has reached the moon, and at the same time is destroying the earth'; a review of Max Nicholson, *The Environmental Revolution*, Hodder and Stoughton). And, 'Warning on survival of mankind' (1969; at a NATO Assembly meeting in Brussels, 'Mankind may have less than a 50–50 chance of surviving till 1980, according to President Nixon's adviser on urban affairs, Dr. Daniel Moynihan'. 'The perils of the modern age are wondrous and protean and, if anything, accumulating', a nuclear holocaust is now 'only the most spectacular of fates' that may be in store for everyone, an 'ecological crisis' is overtaking mankind, and the population trend is 'toward a cultural and biological catastrophe').

These last points have to do with the relationship between human beings and their natural environment or between human beings and things (vehicles, drugs, foods). And they are cogent enough to have prompted a movement away from the concept that dominated the industrialized world for so long – the concept of man-against-nature, man in control of nature and no longer vulnerable to it. Protests against pollution or in favour of conservation, and of course these are not necessarily the same, are more commonplace and more respectable now, but probably the great majority fail to attract international attention, even if they have international implications. That takes something on a bigger scale or with eye-catching 'gimmicks'. Earth Day 1970 in the United States, a 'battle for Earth', had both. It was a nation-wide effort, linking groups with such names as Environment Teach-In Incorporated, Ecology Action, Environment, and Zero Population Growth. Not only students were involved, though they received most of the publicity. Their aim was to draw public attention to the urgency of the problem and set an example in tackling it, e.g. by conserving domestic waste, picketing industrial plants, riding bicyles instead of cars, and practising stringent birth control. The Earth Day programme had some symbolic highlights too, like burying the chassis of a 1970-model car, holding a funeral ceremony for 'the children of tomorrow', and marching on an International Motor Show choking and coughing and wearing black robes, hoods and gas masks. In other words, these were social-reformist protesters rather than retreatist or destruction-oriented pro-testors. And their public demonstration was planned as only one stage in a continuing 'war' against pollution – and 'dehumanization'.

The human opponents in this war were identified as those who claim that there isn't one, or that the battle is unnecessary and unreal: manufacturers whose industrial wastes are disposed of in rivers and coastal waters, politicians who stress the financial rewards to be got from large-scale mining and timber products, and military officials and their scientific advisers who assert that no danger is likely to accrue from atomic experiments, poison and nerve and other gases, disposal of wastes underground or undersea – and so on. The problem of proof is double-headed: 'Who's doing it?' and 'What are the effects?' And it points up the fact that much of what is happening today is actually experimental, although it is not labelled as such: there is no real precedent for it, and no certain means of predicting the outcome.

The same thing applies in the case of other disaster-warnings that bear more directly on inter-human relations.

Automation is not presented as an overwhelming danger to the extent that it used to be, perhaps because so much else has overshadowed it, but it remains relevant. The threat that it posed earlier, of massive retrenchment of all but a few skilled workers in industry (because the existing job structure was not geared to new employment demands and possibilities) has been matched by government claims that a certain proportion of unemployment is normal and good, a sign of a healthy economy. Another kind of menace, also based on machines, has been receiving more attention in the last year or so – in this case, political rather than economic. Some reporters have called it the '1984 threat', because of its potentialities for electronic surveillance of the whole of a nation's population – even, with improved communications between nations, on an almost global scale. The risk to individual privacy is said to lie, first, in the accumulation of specific information being built up in data banks, secondly in the possibilities for electronic eavesdropping and wire-tapping, and thirdly in the combination of these two through interlocking systems – leading to a consolidation of computer-plus-human control and manipulation of large populations and their resources.

And so, to more press headlines: 'A biological revolution' (1969; a conference in California on genetic 'engineering' and its social implications; 'Within 20 years it may be possible to create replicas of living human organisms in a laboratory'; and 'the burning question of the day', 'who would guide those who claim to possess the scientific skills needed to steer mankind?'). 'When machines do the thinking' (1969; a report, from a cybernetics conference in London, 'that the intelligence of machines such as computers was increasing so fast that they would eventually take the place of human brains'). 'Scientists find way to control the human mind' (1969; 'recent advances in research into the chemical control of animal behaviour could ultimately be used by indiscriminate scientists to manipulate large human populations'). 'World Youth Rebellion Inevitable' (1969; report of a U.N. study of world youth problems: 'anti-social behaviour is an inevitable consequence of mankind's developing society', with its increasing urbanization, the 'pressure of mass living', and 'uncertainty about concepts of right and wrong'). 'Rise in violent crime universal – Professor' (1969; Israel Drapkin, Vice-president of the International Society of Criminology, favouring 'English experiments with a new operation which aimed at the removal of certain brain cells of dangerous criminals. This left the criminal a more stable and sensitive person'). And a host of related headings – 'Houses with Top Security' (1969; a new estate near Washington, where house owners have collaborated in a heavily guarded 'walled-village' concept, more stringently policed than similar projects in Florida and California, that 'might set a pattern for nervous American home owners'); accounts of blackboard jungles and concrete jungles, and the 'human jungle' of poverty-ridden areas of large cities; and reports of protective devices for individual use, alarm signals (e.g. 'canned screams') and easy-to-carry weapons like filibusters (New York) which are elegant enough to look like fashion accessories but can be used by women to protect themselves in city streets. Other press features deal with 'Refined horror' (heading of a 1969 review of television programmes), 'Grave-diggers' strike in New York' (1970; 'about 13,000 corpses await burial'), and 'Gangs on Easter Rampage' (1970; 'Teen-age motor cycle gangs of Hell's Angels, rockers and skinheads . . .' in English and Welsh coastal resorts). There are suggestions of new things to come, like 'Artificial islands predicted' (1969; in 20 years' time, floating structures less vulnerable to attack than current land-based settlements; also, 'at the bottom of the seas'), and 'Blue-print created for Moon Creature' (1970; in response to a B.B.C. request for the kind of being that could be designed to live on the moon – the reply being that 'man never could' without protection). And, in a different vein, 'Professor urges sex at school' (1969, 1970; in Hans-Jochen Gamm's book, *Critical School*, suggesting that special classrooms should be 'set aside for pupils to have intercourse undisturbed').

If people accepted all that the press and other mass media tell them, if they took all these warnings and threats and prophecies as being literally and indisputably true, they could reasonably be convinced that there was little future ahead for any of them and even less for their descendants – not in this world, anyway. Perhaps advertising is one factor in reinforcing scepticism as well as inducing belief. (Reports that some United States prisoners of war were able to resist political 'brainwashing' because they had long been habituated to commercial 'brainwashing' appeared to support this notion, but the cause-and-effect sequence has not been adequately demonstrated.) Perhaps science fiction and similar material have 'taken the edge' off some of these warnings so that people have simply become accustomed to them; or the sheer volume of real-life misfortunes, disasters, accidents, crises and wars has dulled the sharpness of their response.

People can, apparently, adjust to a great deal in the way of discomfort and even danger. Examples from all kinds of societies (including the New Guinea highlands), present and past, make this abundantly clear. In any event, possibly because of earlier training in half-belief or outright scepticism, possibly because they are reluctant to take these warnings too seriously, possibly because there is not really much that ordinary individuals can do about many of them, the majority go on for most of the time *as if* they were fictional warnings and not matters of personal urgency. They are used to the 'bad example' as an aspect of everyday fictional dramas. These warnings, then, do not necessarily have the effect of alerting them to action – unless something special triggers it off, or they are convinced (by someone more directly interested or concerned and more influential in guiding opinion) that they can do something to remedy or prevent whatever it is that seems to be going wrong.

Another factor as far as newspaper and other accounts of violent crime, etc., are concerned, and allowing for variable definitions of 'crime' (varying between and even within societies, and through time), is this: that people who pause to think about the topic are able to set current reports in perspective, to some extent, in relation to other places and other times; to realize that such reports come from a far wider regional span than before, and with more immediacy than before; and even to suggest that they are on the whole relatively mild, in nature as well as in quantity, in comparison with what has been and could have been reported in relation to the past.

Qualitatively, many of these themes are as old as human history – and pre-history: examples of aggression and violence, adolescent protest, cruelty, indifference or antagonism to others outside one's own range of reciprocity or interaction, and within it. What is new is the scale on which such events are reported to be taking place, and, especially, the implications for the future in conjunction with warnings about the natural environment. Such warnings also have precedents, of course.

In some cases they are set within a cyclical conception of rebirth and renewal – as in the Hindu view of cyclical destruction and re-creation of the entire universe at the end of each *kalpa*, a kalpa being one small part of the overall division into four world ages, or yuga (the present age being Kali Yuga, or Kali Yug, the age of iron as contrasted with the age of gold, a time of pessimism and the predominance of evil).* The Buddhist 'Four Ages' conception contains cyclical elements, but they are much less salient: we are currently in the Third Age, with the age of the Maitreya, the Buddha-to-come, still some time in the future – and the final outcome is Nirvana, the ultimate dissolution. And Christian views of Armageddon (given block headings, at intervals, in the religious sections of some newspapers), the millennium, the coming of the Messiah, and so on, are directly linear in orientation.

More traditional prophecies of disaster, doom and catastrophe, heralding major changes – on earth, or as a transition to another world – in these and other frameworks, virtually all have to do with religious or supernatural conceptions: actions taken by deities or supernatural beings, laws set in motion by them, and so on. Current prophecies, however, include a growing emphasis on what human beings can do in this direction: the possibility that man through his own efforts, not simply through invoking or displeasing a deity or through a mechanical breach of a religious tabu, can bring about the physical destruction of the entire world and its inhabitants.

This is itself a radical departure from traditional views. And it is within this context that attempts are now being made to bring together again two dimensions that had been more or less artificially separated: the dimension of man in relation to natural environment, and the dimension of man in relation to

* For a useful brief account, see H. Zimmer, edited by J. Campbell, *Myths and Symbols in Indian Art and Civilization*, Harper, New York (Harper Torchbooks), 1962 (1st published 1946), pp. 13–19.

man. The implications for research, and disseminating the results of research, are obvious.

With the widening scale of human affairs (improved communications, transport and so on), the 'broad sweep' approach becomes increasingly more imperative, to set localized and highly detailed accounts in broader perspective. At the same time, it is increasingly less satisfactory, more open to question. There is so much ground to be covered, that exceptions tend to be glossed over. There is room for the 'Yes, but . . .' of protest, but not for the 'Yes, but . . .' of careful qualification and sifting of evidence, except in a somewhat specialized context. The smaller the communication network, the more specific the messages can be. To reach a wider public, the picture must be drawn more sharply. This does not eliminate controversy – on the contrary, perhaps. It does mean that there is not the same room for deliberation on details, or for balancing between opposing views: that there is more pressure to take a stand, for or against, without necessarily being in a position to present, or to have access to, all or most of the relevant evidence.

The kaleidoscope of mixed information that makes up the content of communication, both 'mass' and interpersonal, includes repetition, rebuttal, reframing, misreading and mis-representation of what has already been said by others. And exposure to all of this accumulated information is uneven: it is not spread uniformly throughout a society. Socio-cultural learning continues to be a slow process. For human beings, there is no way of acquiring instant access to a large accumula-tion of 'knowledge' or arriving at an instant assessment of it. The enormous improvement in storage facilities, made possible through computers, has not been matched by improvement in the means of transmitting this material.

Newspaper headings have gone so far as to cry 'Print Pollution!' The same sentiment is echoed in complaints of even the most avid readers in the social sciences (for instance), to the effect that they can't keep up with what is being written even in their particular subfields. The congestion is most obvious in regard to journals; 'abstracts' of 'abstracts', and 'digests' of 'digests', add to the volume rather than diminishing it. Some scientists 'seem to have surrendered and . . . are now relying largely on word of mouth for the communication of ideas. The popularity of seminars, colloquia, conferences . . . is indicative of this.'* The trend was already evident a couple of decades ago, but the suggestions made then for coping with the 'print explosion' did not go much further than the unsatisfactory remedy of microfilms.

Current answers are being sought in the computer, as a means of circulating as well as storing information.† But in the more specialized areas of the social and other sciences and in the wider fields outside them, this does not, and will not in the immediate future, obviate the need for human intermediaries. Problems of selection and context-of-presentation continue to be relevant. The mass media, for instance, define various situations for their publics in a number of ways, and not simply through what they say directly – or refrain from saying. In some cases, this selective bias is fairly readily identifiable, such as when a reader or listener or viewer can make comparisons and is able to see that one feature is highlighted as against another. But mostly it is not so easy. In reported interviews, the framing of questions – what is asked, and how – can affect the response (a point that social scientists are

* A. F. Gurnett-Smith, 'The Interface between Science and Society', *The Australian Journal of Science*, Vol. 32, No. 4, 1969, p. 144.

† See, for example, an editorial note (signed K.S.) in the *American Sociological Review*, Vol. 35, No. 2, 1970, facing p. 201, reporting on 'the proposal of the American Psychological Association's policy and planning board to establish a national information service for psychology', a proposal noted in *Science*, Vol. 167, 1970, p. 1228.

expected to bear in mind in carrying out research): but while there are some checks on this in a situation with which a reader (etc.) is familiar, they become progressively less effective outside it. The selection of 'world news', for instance, ranges all the way from local editors' arrangement and choice of material (and headlines) to the distant man-on-the-spot who must obtain and transmit it. Radio and television commentaries such as 'Notes on the news' are designed to amplify and explain what is happening at home and abroad: 'Our correspondents report . . .', etc. – and so we have more words, to a point perhaps where fewer people are prepared to listen to them.

Among all these words, these voices competing for attention, some speak more loudly and more insistently than others. Commercial advertising reinforces other verbal pressures that emphasize, not only the ever-increasing accumulation (or, at least, purchasing) of goods, but also individual freedom and individual choice, expressed through self-indulgence and personal gratification. ('Why don't you go down to . . . and have a good time?' 'You owe yourself a holiday!' 'Give yourself a treat!' Or, in an Australian Post Office advertisement, as one of a cluster of similar appeals, 'Ring the babysitter and take the day off. You deserve it' – this last under a huge caption with a smaller inset below, 'Make Something Happen! Talk is cheap.') The voices of organized religion are less dominating than they were,* although still important. Politics, and 'intellectual' points of view, are recognized as being committed to partisan positions – or suspected of being so, where these are not overtly expressed: the influence of Marx, Karl Mannheim, and the sociology of knowledge is pervasive, as well as specific.

Science alone was for a long time hailed as a neutral area,

* See, for example, B. R. Wilson, *Sects and Society. A Sociological comment*, Watts, 1966.

ideally not tied to pre-existing claims of rank and privilege, and a source and means of bringing material benefits to all mankind. But if 'science' is neutral, scientists are not: and the question of how to cope with this human quality of personal involvement, the social science dilemma, has no 'right' answers.

When does a person put forward an opinion as a social scientist and not just as a citizen presenting a personal point of view? He can make really authoritative pronouncements only in the particular field, and on the topic, where he has undisputed competence – and that range is likely to be quite small. What is more, there is a tendency in formal academic psychology and sociology to restrict the notion of competence to findings that are statistically significant. But it is important to remember that this need not mean they are *substantively* significant.*

A few years ago, arguments raged about the distinction between qualitative and quantitative emphases in social science research. One question was whether everything in socio-cultural living could be satisfactorily quantified, especially in the field of aesthetics – songs, poetry, art, and so on. Some held that, while opinions, attitudes, etc., could be measured, this did not apply to the *content* of such material, because appropriate units of measurement were not easy to define. This particular argument has not so much died down, as changed direction. It has merged into a more general issue: the need to match research problems with the procedures and techniques that are most appropriate to them, and greater sophistication in the use, and relevance, of statistics. As in the case of physical anthropology, simple measurement is no

---

* L. Kish drew attention to the difference between these two kinds of 'significance', which are too often identified, in 'Some Statistical Problems in Research Design', *American Journal of Sociology*, Vol. 24, No. 3, 1959.

longer adequate: the focus now is on relations between items and not on individual items as such.

One danger, however, in tying the notion of confidence too closely to *statistical* significance, is that some research workers are wary of choosing research topics that are not easily quantifiable. If science is 'the prediction business', and prediction is difficult enough at any time, so the argument runs, it can rest only on small, definitive studies where variables can be effectively controlled: in the larger arena, prediction is almost impossible, and all one can say is, 'In such and such a case, given this and that, the outcome is likely to be . . .', or, 'this outcome is more likely than that'. For people in search of certainties, this is not enough: and it is not enough for some scientists themselves, including social scientists. When it comes to involvement in affairs outside their own particular professional fields, by way of active intervention or acting as guides (or prophets) to others, non-scientific factors come into play. These find expression, for instance, in action on the basis of emotional commitment (faith, belief); it may be purely instrumental, attempting to achieve certain ends that are more or less clearly specified, but it almost certainly involves some measure of expressive action too. Alternatively, they may find expression in refusal to act, on the grounds that (*a*) 'It's not our business', other people have a right to 'do their own thing' without interference; (*b*) Decisions on 'good' and 'bad', 'right' and 'wrong', are outside their control: 'Who is to say what's good . . .?' etc.; 'It depends on the context'; 'It's OK in that particular subculture' or environment, so why should I intervene?'; (*c*) 'Anyway, we *can't* intervene; we have no access to the channels of power and authority; anything we can do will only touch the surface'; or (*d*) We don't know enough about the situation to predict the likely consequences, even tentatively; we can ask questions, but we can't even sketch in possible answers.

An enormous amount has been written about the place of 'values' in social science (Weber, Myrdal, Nadel, etc.).* And because there is no simple solution and a great deal of uncertainty, plus substantial and virtually intransigent disagreement, the problem comes up undiminished with each generation of social scientists.

Nehru, in opening the 46th Indian Science Congress, spoke (in 1959) of science itself in the symbolic language of myth. 'Having banished many gods before which men bowed, science had itself assumed a godlike face. Like the Janus, the god of the month of January, science had two faces, the face of the creator and the face of the destroyer. "Both faces look down on us and we have to make a choice which face we like". . .' But alongside the use of specific, conscious metaphors and analogies (i.e. the deliberate use of symbolic language), and underlying the manifestations of formal, institutionalized religion, mythical thinking persists in the field of scientific inquiry as elsewhere in human socio-cultural life.

Contrasts are sometimes drawn between, say, Australian Aborigines and their myths on one hand, Western-type society with its space equipment and computers on the other. These contrasts still have a strong popular appeal, and find substantial support in the classificatory schemes we looked at in Chapter 2. It is true that some of those who propound and support them qualify them with such statements as, 'We acknowledge that in Western civilization there are immense differences between scientists and ordinary laymen.' But for practical purposes this, so to speak, cuts no ice: and people

---

* Robert Lynd's short statement of a few years ago is still interesting in this connection: *Knowledge for What? The Place of Social Science in American Culture*, Princeton University Press, 1939. And, for a contrast, R. L. Warren, 'Toward a Non-Utopian Normative Model of the Community', *American Sociological Review*, Vol. 35, No. 2, 1970, pp. 219–28, e.g. p. 219.

who themselves have a minimum of formal education and even, in some instance, a minimum of technical skills, continue to regard themselves as civilized, Australian Aborigines and other traditionally non-literate, 'tribal' peoples as uncivilized, barbarian, even savage.

C. P. Snow's distinction of a few years ago, between the 'two cultures' of science and of letters, has been modified and subdivided from various angles: but one that is especially relevant to us here is the division, admittedly blurred, between science and technology – or between scientists and technologists.* Even Gordon Childe, optimistic as he was about human progress as a long-term prospect despite short-term ups-and-downs, admitted that technological developments were more striking and more convincing than achievements in other spheres of living. Ogburn† asserted that there was a cultural lag, or disjunction, between material and non-material aspects of culture, the material progressing at a pace too fast for social relations and other, less tangible, elements to make the necessary adjustments. Lévy-Bruhl, although in his earlier work he exaggerated the prevalence of, as he called it, 'pre-logical' thought among non-literate peoples, admitted later that this was a widespread, and common human attribute. His findings in this respect would have been confirmed, had he lived to continue his inquiries today.

Anthropologists, among others, have long advocated the need for study of a wide range of socio-cultural 'answers' to pan-human problems (see Chapter 1), but they have also had reservations about the circumstances in which this may be done. A society or a culture can be studied simply in order to

---

* See for example, A. F. Gurnett-Smith, ibid., p. 143.

† W. F. Ogburn and M. F. Nimkoff, *Sociology*, Houghton Mifflin, Boston, 1950 (2nd ed.). This belongs within the area of 'social function' studies, long associated with such divergent names as Boas, Malinowski, and Robert Merton.

destroy it more effectively – and there are many examples, from missionary enterprises to military ones. Also, some senior anthropologists consistently opposed the idea of having their subject introduced into schools, even at the secondary level, because they had reservations on the score of moral values. They were apprehensive about the possible influence of differing views of right and wrong, on children who had not yet come to terms with the norms and values of their own social environment.

Of course, this question has been bypassed in one sense, magnified in another, through the effects of the mass media – which have intensified the ordinary processes of cross-cultural communication and borrowing. And these have coincided with developments in the social sciences, where ethnographic studies of other cultures and of 'one's own' culture, even if presented in a neutral framework ('this is what happens'), have had the effect of legitimizing the activities and the norms that they describe. In looking at 'street corner societies' and other 'gang' situations, for instance, it became fashionable, not merely to delineate social structure as a routine part of an inquiry, but to emphasize that structure was there – that gangs, etc., were structured, and had their own norms and values which were 'legitimate for them'. And so, in a way, we have cultural relativism turned inward upon itself, as a force to be reckoned with, within societies and not only between them. The recognition and *de facto* legitimation of subcultural norms has far-reaching implications for social cohesion: the old problem of the individual versus society, once dismissed as irrelevant in modern social scientific analysis, has proved to be very much alive in this new context.

Views differ as to whether modern society is becoming more diverse or more uniform than it was a few years ago; but, of course, it is both.* And both are equally obtrusive. The pro-

* See, for example, R. M. Berndt, 'The Other End of the Telescope',

liferation of protests and actions of dissent is particularly obvious, perhaps, because they ramify through all parts of a society and are not restricted to any one section or class or regional quarter within it, and also because they represent trouble-cases, items of news. So are reports of hippies and skinheads, rockers and surfies, bikies, skippies (who 'skip' without paying rent, etc.), diggers (who burn or eat paper money and believe in 'giving everything away'), religious sects like the Hare Krishnas and the Jesus Freaks (with their slogan, 'Jesus is Better than Dope'): 'drop-outs', people who 'opt out' of a society and refuse to admit responsibility to or for any part of it, and those who are actively, even passionately, involved in trying to change it for the better ('the better', variously defined). The message that comes over the mass media is quite often, in effect, 'savagery begins at home': and for large sections of the population in many societies, even today, and including the so-called civilized world, the normal state of affairs is aptly summarized in Marett's description of 'savagery'* as one of 'intellectual confusion combined with physical discomfort'. The diminishing of the emotional security that many once found in organized religion has not done away with the search for something comparable, in here-and-now terms (the demand for 'instant prosperity', e.g. strikes and wage claims and football pools as a secular equivalent of Melanesian cargo cults), or in magico-religious belief and ritual (e.g. the 1968 effort of a group of 'hippies' to move St Pancras railway station across the Thames to Bermondsey, through prayers and invocations).

For Durkheim, the danger to society – specifically, the

The Australian Journal of Science, Vol. 25, No. 4, 1962, pp. 146–55; this looks at the concept of the 'exotic' in a number of societies, as contrasted with the bleaching activities of the mythical Mother Sereda in James Branch Cabell's novel *Jurgen* (Penguin Books, 1940, p. 36).

* R. R. Marett, *Man in the Making . . .*, Benn, 1927/28, p. 8.

society of France in his day – lay in the breakdown of the
moral rules that governed relations between its members, to a
point where emphasis on individual self-interest threatened
the entire fabric of co-operation on which it rested. For
Cassirer, the danger to human beings in general lay in the
non-rational, the emotional: in mythical thinking, which
strengthened the cohesion of believers, but at the expense of
the wider social context – and at the expense of 'the process of
man's progressive self-liberation' through the help of language,
art, religion and science.* In this context, then, the Greek
Myth – as an ideal statement of the beginnings of lucid,
rational inquiry – has both substance and relevance. Ralph
Linton, writing in the shade of the approaching second
World War, dedicated his book, *The Study of Man*, to 'the
next civilization' because he saw no place in the immediate
future for the kind of research that characterized the social
sciences. He compared the situation of European civilization
then to that of the Alexandrine Greeks who were the last
direct descendants, culturally speaking, of the classical Greek
tradition: they were not able to follow up their own, early
scientific developments, but their heritage could none the less
be passed on to others; and Linton, with mixed pessimism
and optimism, hoped that the same would eventually apply
to the scientific achievements of contemporary Europe. As
against that are the 'no future' prophecies of the press headlines, and the despair that is frequently voiced in reference to a
host of social situations, formal or otherwise. This note of
despair is well put in a book review which, although dealing
specifically with New York city, has much wider implications: 'Too many people are trying to help in too many ways.
New pressure groups emerge, only to subdivide and fragment;
new projects are mooted, only to collide with some vested

* *An Essay on Man* . . ., Doubleday Anchor, New York, 1954 (1st
published 1944), p. 286.

interest, ideological, economic or bureaucratic. Every kind of social expert is on hand, endless conferences are held, and, if anything, the condition of the poor grows worse. The problem is too large and slippery, the various factions too inflexible, the racial and social bitterness too deeply fixed. No paternalistic solution is possible, and the victims themselves seem more inclined to self-destruction than sustained self-help. The city is simply ungovernable.'*

And, on the religious side, an example of one guideline that uses the past to prophesy for the future – a press advertisement (1969) for a religious meeting:

Why blame youth! / THE WORLD AFLAME. / Lust-Crime-Violence-Lawlessness. / This is the generation of race-hatred, free-love, new morality and the youth revolt. With unbelief, sex-mania, and the rocketing crime-rate, what is our society coming to? / Are we being taken for a trip, OR ARE WE GOING TO POT? / Thoughtful people keep asking – / Why all this chaos? / Can the mad world be stopped? / Where will it end? / UNKNOWN to millions and overlooked by thousands the Bible shows an amazing solution. / HEAR – H.J.B. – reveal the positive answer to these perplexing problems. / SEE – Candid pictures from the world's centres of modernity, and also pictures of the fun-loving city of Pompeii.

We began this discussion by looking at some of the things that had been said about the place of Greece and Rome in the world of today, as the zone of distant but linked traditions from which western Europe traces its main, though by no means its only, lines of descent. That led, almost inevitably, to a consideration of the notion of civilization and related ways of classifying human societies and cultures.

Then we turned to two peoples who, because they have been categorized as standing 'outside history', have been

* In B. Nightingale's Review of *The Bag* (by S. Yurick, Gollancz), in 'Uptown and downtown', *The Observer Review*, London, 10 January 1970, p. 33.

relegated to an obscure corner of the literature on the ways of mankind, or no corner at all. These too-brief accounts concentrated on a facet of their cultures which could be presented fairly simply, without the detailed explanations that would have been necessary for a more comprehensive understanding of them. It is not that intellectual inquiry is, or was traditionally, lacking in these cultures: but such inquiry is set within a mythical framework, based upon mythical premises (as so much intellectual inquiry has been, and is, in many other societies too). To explore this would have led us too deeply into the sphere of myth, and of language categories – and into the social dimension as well. In the Aboriginal chapter, we sank a small shaft part of the way into this social dimension, in one area, to indicate the kind of basic information that would need to be mastered before any study in depth could begin.

Talking about verbal imagery on the edges of religious symbolism, without becoming caught up in consideration of religious symbolism itself, nevertheless meant that we had to look a little more closely at myth, outlining a number of points of view on it. And so to the mass media, as a means of purveying mythical and other material, and some of the issues associated with them; and on to one area of symbolic language in Western society today, also outside the field of organized religion, the area, specifically, of cartoons and advertising.

The interplay between conservatism and change in this area took us back to the question of civilization, in relation to such concepts as modernization, to eschatological press headlines, and to the decline in unquestioning acceptance of the formal authority of institutionalized religious leaders, and also of faith in the leaders whose access to the 'scientific mystique' had been surrounding them with an aura of sanctification. Outside the narrow range of reasonably accurate prediction, then, where are the *other* prophets – the guides who will assist ordinary citizens to deal with the accumulating mass of information from so many sources and sift it for truth or falsity, relevance or irrelevance? In Red Riding Hood terms, who will help them to find a way through (or, out of) the wood? If, as Braidwood put it (see Chapter 2), most of mankind is now engrossed in the third act of a play, which may or may not destroy it (whereas the non-literate, tribal world was previously left behind in the first act), the question is, what is the fourth act? Or will it be a new play altogether, with a different script? There have always been people to claim that what went on in non-literate societies could have no possible bearing on the 'civilized' life of urban Europeans. Likewise, there are many now who profess to see no relevance at all in the events of the past – in any society, including their own. The future, they say, will be so very different that blueprints from the past can provide no guide to it at all. And some current prophets, mainly educators, have advocated forcefully that children growing up now should be prepared, not just for the unexpected, but for the 'unimaginable'.

For any given society, the 'outsiders' on its regional and linguistic and cultural borders represent a potential threat, even if they offer other advantages – in trade, for instance, or as intermediaries in communication with more distant peoples, or simply as fighting partners or someone to 'identify against'. They are foreigners who don't speak the same language or observe the same customs and rules. But they are also sources of new ideas as well as goods. And even in the conventional picture of civilizations overrun by barbarians – a picture to which cultural relativism, not necessarily under that name, has been according a revised label – these invasions and massive disturbances proved, in the long term, to be invigorating and revitalizing influences. The Mongols, for example, are now being shown to have enriched the art and culture of both Europe and China – as a positive, not a negative force in the history of those regions.

But the process of reinvigoration can be a painful one and its outcome entirely uncertain – a 'modernizing', not necessarily a 'civilizing' process. The 'barbarians within' can offer as much of a threat as the 'barbarians without': the groups within a society that don't speak the same language, literally or figuratively, reject established norms, and endeavour to substitute these with their own – or simply to overthrow them. Pejorative connotations aside, from one standpoint the reformist-protestors might be compared with the revitalizing 'barbarians' of the Old World, prodding a society into reviewing its rules and its practices, forcing it into a more thoughtful assessment of its internal and external relations. The 'drop-outs' and negative rejectors, in contrast, could well be equated with the destructive aspect of the barbarian onslaughts. But, whether or not this is a useful way of looking at it, the dialogue between 'civilization' and 'barbarians' is a continuing process, one that is relevant to all human societies – because ultimately it is concerned with the problem of social order, social cohesion, and social integrity; and this is something that is always 'in process', a matter of more or less, whether the societies involved are Australian Aboriginal or New Guinean or the larger social and national units of the Western world.

Suggestions for Further Reading

These lists do not include all the references noted in the main text. They are quite selective, but endeavour to give a fairly wide coverage; and references noted in most of these works provide additional sources.

Chapter 1
The Penguin-Pelican series on facets of Greek and Roman Civilization, including translations, is probably the best introduction to this topic: H. Kitto, *The Greeks*, J. Balsdon, ed., *Roman Civilization*, J. Boardman's *The Greeks Overseas*, C. M. Bowra, *Landmarks in Greek Literature*, etc.; also, for example, *The Twelve Olympians, Gods and Goddesses of Greece: A modern View of Ancient Myths*, Pan Books, 1952. Anthropological references, on cross-cultural perspective, are noted under Chapters 2–3.

Chapters 2 and 3
Glyn Daniel, *The Idea of Prehistory*, Watts, 1962, and *The First Civilizations. The Archaeology of their Origins*, Thames and Hudson, 1968; R. J. Braidwood, *Prehistoric Men*, Scott, Foresman and Co., Glenview, Ill., 1967 (7th ed.; previous eds. published by the Field Museum of Natural History); Gordon Childe's books, including *What happened in History?* Penguin Books, 1967 ed. (first published 1942); T. W. Wallbank *et al.*, *Civilization Past and Present*, 2 vols., Scott, Foresman and Co., Glenview, Ill., 1969; C. L. Riley, *The Origins of Civilization*, Southern Illinois University Press, Carbondale,

Ill., Feffer and Simons, London, 1969; M. Melko, *The Nature of Civilizations*, Porter Sargent, Boston, 1969; and A. Toynbee's voluminous works, including *Civilization on Trial*, Oxford University Press, 1953 (first published 1946); M. F. Ashley Montagu, ed., *The Concept of the Primitive*, Free Press, New York; Collier-Macmillan, London, 1968; J. H. Beattie, *Other Cultures*, Cohen and West, London, 1964; R. Firth, *Human Types*, Nelson, 1956, and *Elements of Social Organization*, Watts, 1951; A. Dundes, ed., *Every Man His Way. Readings in Cultural Anthropology*, Prentice-Hall, Englewood Cliffs, N. J., 1968; R. L. Beals and H. Hoijer, *An Introduction to Anthropology*, Macmillan, New York, 1956 (first published 1953); J. Honigmann, *The World of Man*, Harper and Bros., New York, 1959; M. Herskovits, *Man and his Works*, Knopf, New York, 1949 (first published 1947). Other references are noted in the text. See also, for preliminary reading, M. Singer, ed., *Introducing India in Liberal Education*, Proceedings of a Conference held at the University of Chicago, Chicago University Press, 1957; H. G. Creel, ed., *Chinese Civilization in Liberal Education*, Proceedings of a Conference held at the University of Chicago, 1958, Chicago University Press, 1959. On Polynesian voyages, see the *Journal of the Polynesian Society*, which includes a number of relevant articles and book reviews.

Chapter 4

For a short preliminary account, see our *The First Australians*, Ure Smith, Sydney, 1952/1969, and, for a more detailed general coverage, *The World of the First Australians*, Ure Smith, Sydney, 1964/1968. (This includes a bibliography.) We discuss myth and social relations, among other things, in a volume on the western side of Arnhem Land: *Man, Land and Myth in North Australia. The Gunwinggu People*, also Ure Smith, 1970. A brief statement on myth, etc., is C. H. Berndt, 'The Arts of Life, an Australian Aboriginal Perspective', *Westerly*, Vol. 1, Nos. 1–2, 1952. Some particularly attractive song and myth translations are contained in T. G. H. Strehlow's *Aranda Traditions*, Melbourne University Press, 1947, and in his 1972 volume *Songs of Central Australia* (Angus and Robertson, Sydney). Other references: A. P. Elkin. *The Australian Aborigines . . .*, Angus and Robertson, Sydney, 1938/1965; W. L. Warner,

A Black Civilization, Harper, New York, 1937/1958; P. Kaberry, *Aboriginal Woman, Sacred and Profane*, Routledge, 1939; R. M. and C. H. Berndt, eds., *Aboriginal Man in Australia*, Angus and Robertson, Sydney, 1965; L.R. Hiatt, *Kinship and Conflict*, The Australian National University, Canberra, 1965; W. E. H. Stanner, *After the Dreaming*, Australian Broadcasting Commission, Sydney, 1969; M. Meggitt, *Desert People*, Angus and Robertson, Sydney, 1962. Also articles in the journal *Oceania*, now published by the University of Sydney.

Chapter 5

The *New Guinea Encyclopaedia*, to be published in 1972 by the Melbourne University Press, covers a very wide range of topics, including a section on Mythology and Oral Literature by C. H. Berndt and one on Social Control by R. M. Berndt. Other more specific studies are F. E. Williams, *Drama of Orokolo. The Social and Ceremonial Life of the Elema*, Oxford at the Clarendon Press, 1940; K. O. L. Burridge, *Tangu Traditions* (same press), 1969; R. M. Berndt, *Excess and Restraint. Social Control among a New Guinea Mountain People*, Chicago University Press, 1962; M. Reay, *The Kuma . . .*, Melbourne University Press, 1959; J. van Baal, *Dema . . .*, Martinus Nijhoff, The Hague, 1966; P. Lawrence and M. Meggitt, eds., *Gods, Ghosts and Men in Melanesia*, Oxford University Press, Melbourne, 1965; and Malinowski's works on the Trobriands, such as *Argonauts of The Western Pacific*, Routledge and Kegan Paul, 1922 (reprinted 1966), and *The Sexual Life of Savages*, Routledge, 1939. On 'cargo cults', etc., see P. Worsley, *The Trumpet Shall Sound*, MacGibbon and Kee, 1957; K. Burridge, *Mambu: A Melanesian Millennium*, Methuen, 1960; P. Lawrence, *Road Belong Cargo*, Manchester University Press, 1964; also N. Cohn, *The Pursuit of the Millennium*, Paladin Books, London, 1970 (revised ed.; first published 1957). Also articles in, for example, the journals *Oceania* and *Anthropological Forum*.

Chapter 7

B. Malinowski, *Myth in Primitive Psychology*, Doubleday, New York, 1954 (first published 1926) is a classic study, but needs to be read critically. C. Kluckholn, 'Recurrent Themes in Myths and Mythmaking', in H. A. Murray, ed. *Myth and Mythmaking*, George

Braziller, New York, 1960; E. Cassirer, e.g. *Language and Myth*, Harper, New York, Dover Books, 1946 (first published in German) and *The Myth of the State*, Yale University Press, New Haven, 1950 (first published 1946); T. Sebeok, ed., *Myth: a Symposium*, American Folklore Society, Philadelphia, 1955, includes articles on several topics, including 'truth–falsity': on the last, see also D. Bidney, *Theoretical Anthropology*, Columbia University Press, New York, 1953; R. Gotesky, 'The Nature of Myth and Society', *American Anthropologist*, Vol. 54, No. 4, 1952, and D. H. Hymes and I. Wassermann, 'On the Nature of Myth: an Analysis of Some Recent Criticism', ibid., Vol. 55, No. 3, 1953; *Myth: a Symposium* also contains an article by C. Lévi-Strauss on 'The Structural Study of Myth'; his other works include *Mythologiques, Le Cru et Le Cuit* and *Mythologiques, Du Miel aux Cendres*, both published by Plon, Paris (1964 and 1966); see also E. Leach, ed., *The Structural Study of Myth and Totemism*, Tavistock, 1967: Part I, on Myth; and M. Lane, ed., *Structuralism, a Reader*, Cape, 1970. Also, B. Colby, 'Cultural Patterns in Narrative', *Science*, Vol. 151, pp. 793–8, 1966, and 'The Analysis of Culture Content and the Patterning of Narrative Concern in Texts', *American Anthropologist*, Vol. 68, No. 2, 1966; and articles in J. Greenway, ed., *The Anthropologist Looks at Myth*, Texas University Press, Austin, including C. H. Berndt, 'The Ghost Husband . . .'. On symbols, see, for example, S. F. Nadel, *The Foundations of Social Anthropology*, Cohen and West, London, 1951, and C. Morris, *Signs, Language and Behaviour*, Prentice-Hall, New York, 1946. On Rama and Ravana, see, for example, M. Singer, 'The Cultural Pattern of Indian Civilization', *Far Eastern Quarterly*, Vol. XV, No. 1, 1955, and P. Dolaphilla, in R. Pieris, ed., *Some Aspects of Traditional Sinhalese Culture*, report of a conference at the University of Ceylon, Peradeniya, 1956. For examples of psychoanalytic interpretation, see J. Campbell, *The Hero with a Thousand Faces*, Meridian Books, Cleveland, Ohio, 1967 (first published 1949); C. G. Jung and K. Kerényi, trans. R. Hull, *Introduction to a Science of Mythology . . .*, Routledge and Kegan Paul, 1951 (1st English ed.). On folktales, Stith Thompson, *The Folktale*, Dryden Press, N.Y., 1946; also, in T. Sebeok, ed., op. cit., 1955. A fairly wide-ranging overview in reference to 'folktales' is J. Fischer, 'The Sociopsychological Study of

Myths and Folktales', *Current Anthropology*, Vol. 4, No. 3, 1963.

Chapter 8

B. Rosenberg and D. M. White, eds., *Mass Culture*, Free Press of Glencoe, New York, 1957, is a useful introduction (paperback ed. 1964); also, M. Albrecht, 'The Relationship of Literature and Society', *American Journal of Sociology*, Vol. LIX, No. 5, 1954, and 'Does Literature Reflect Common Values?' *American Sociological Review*, Vol. 21, No. 6, 1956; J. T. Klapper, *The Effects of Mass Communication*, Free Press, New York, 1960; W. Albig, *Modern Public Opinion*, McGraw-Hill, New York, 1956 (rev. ed.); W. A. Belson, *The Impact of Television. Methods and Findings in Program Research*, Crosby Lockwood, 1967; O. N. Larsen, ed., *The Effects of the Mass Media*, Harper and Row, 1968; C. Hovland, *et al.*, *Communication and Persuasion*, Yale University Press, New Haven, 1953; E. Casty, ed., *Mass Media and Mass Man*, Holt, Rinehart and Winston, New York, 1968; T. Peterson and J. Jensen, *The Mass Media and Modern Society*, Holt, Rinehart and Winston, New York, 1965; T. Shibutani, *Improved News; a Sociological Study of Rumour*, Bobbs-Merrill, 1966; H. Wilensky, 'Mass Society and Mass Culture: Interdependence or Independence', in E. H. Mizruchi, ed., *The Substance of Sociology*, Appleton-Century-Crofts, New York, 1967 (reprinted from the *American Sociological Review*, Vol. 29, 1964); R. Denny, *The Astonished Muse*, University of Chicago Press, 1957; L. H. Streicher, 'David Low and the Sociology of Caricature', *Comparative Studies in Society and History*, Volume VIII, No. 1, 1965; G. Parry and A. Aldridge, *The Penguin Book of Comics*, Penguin Books, 1967; V. Eller, *The Mad Morality: or the Ten Commandments Revisited*, Abingdon Press, 1970; and, for cartoon examples, J. Chase *et al.*, *Today's Cartoon*, foreword by R. McGill, The Hauser Press, New Orleans, 1962. M. McLuhan, *Understanding Media: The Extensions of Man*. Sphere Books, London, 1967/1968 (first published 1964); McLuhan and Q. Fiore, *The Medium is the Massage*, Bantam Books, New York, 1967; R. Short, *The Parables of Peanuts*, Collins, Fontana Books, 1968 (also *The Gospel according to Peanuts*, 1965), and F. C. Crews, *The Pooh Perplex. A Freshman Casebook*, Dutton Paperback, New York, 1965 (first published 1964). And A. Walker, *Sex in the Movies*,

Penguin Books, 1968 (Chapters 8 and 9, on censorship). K. Burke's work, e.g. *A Grammar of Motives*, *A Rhetoric of Motives* and *Language and Symbolic Action*, University of California Press, is also relevant here.

Chapter 9
B. Rosenberg and D. M. White, eds., *Mass Culture*, Free Press of Glencoe, New York, 1957, is useful here too; also such journals as the *Journal of Advertising Research*, New York. S. H. Britt, ed., *Consumer Behavior and the Behavioral Sciences*, Wiley, New York, 1966, is a useful introduction to a variety of topics and references in this field; D. B. Lucas and S. H. Britt, *Advertising Psychology and Research. An Introductory Book*, McGraw-Hill, New York, 1950; E. S. Turner, *The Shocking History of Advertising*, Penguin Books, 1965 (first published 1952); M. Mayer, *Madison Avenue, U.S.A.*, Penguin Books, 1961 (first published 1958); and Vance Packard, e.g. *The Hidden Persuaders*, Penguin Books, 1960 (first published 1957) and *The Waste-Makers*, Penguin Books, 1967 (first published 1960). See also L. Mumford, *Technics and Civilization*, Routledge, 1947 (first published 1934). And D. Thompson, ed., *Discrimination and Popular Culture*, Penguin Books, 1970 (first published 1964), and J. Russell and S. Gablik, eds., *pop art redefined*, Thames & Hudson, 1969.

Chapter 10
See, for example, W. F. Ogburn and M. F. Nimkoff, *Sociology*, Houghton Mifflin, Boston, 1950 (2nd edition), and the discussion of 'culture lag' in this by R. Bierstedt, *The Social Order ...*, McGraw Hill, New York, 1963 (first published 1957). R. Redfield, *The Primitive World and its Transformations*, Cornell University Press, Ithaca, 1953, and Penguin (Peregrine) Books, 1968; R. Merton, *Social Theory and Social Structure*, Free Press, Glencoe, Ill., 1957 (or later editions). R. P. Cuzzort, *Humanity and Modern Sociological Thought*, Holt, Rinehart, New York, 1969; G. Hardin, Introd., *Science, Conflict and Society*, Readings from *Scientific American*, 1969; J. Nuttall, *Bomb Culture*, Paladin Books, London, 1970; J. R. Gusfield, ed. *Protest, Reform, and Revolt. A Reader in Social Movements*, Wiley, New York, 1970; S. N. Eisenstadt, *Modernization: Protest and Change*, Prentice-Hall, Englewood Cliffs, N.J., 1966.

Index

ELITES AND SOCIETY

T. B. Bottomore

Every society has its elite – from the least-developed jungle tribe with its hereditary warrior chiefs to the great modern civilizations with their political, industrial and financial power-pyramids. The elitists – social theorists, who have examined the workings of societies in terms of their minority elite groups – have had an important influence on modern sociology.

This book is a survey of the principal elitist theories, from Mosca and Pareto to C. Wright Mills and Raymond Aron. It distinguishes between the theoretical and ideological elements in such theories, and reviews as well some of the principal experimental studies of elite groups both in advanced and in underdeveloped countries.

Finally, it considers some questions of social philosophy which arise from a confrontation of the idea of elites with the ideas of democracy and social equality.

PRIMITIVE GOVERNMENT

Lucy Mair

We take so much for granted the familiar forms of government – parliament, cabinet, ministries, law courts, and local authorities – that we are apt to forget which features constitute the essential elements of rule. These become clearer when we study how government has evolved to suit the needs of family, tribe, nation, and even empire.

Professor Mair has carried out field work on various widely differing systems which, in spite of the imposition of colonial rule, still in part obtain in East Africa. In these primitive societies it would appear that concepts of law and government were already understood and developed. In fact Professor Mair contends, contrary to some previous opinions, that no known society exists without them, even though their forms may be rudimentary.

Some such systems are quite outside the experience of western readers. For instance, an apparent anarchy may prove, on examination, to be in reality a well-ordered kind of government. In one society political responsibility is diffused throughout the whole; in another men have built up a kingdom which could be compared to those of medieval Europe.

In this survey of the way in which government is conducted without modern technical equipment, Professor Mair throws much new light on its historical evolution.